INDIANS

AND

OTHER AMERICANS

INDIANS
AND
OTHER AMERICANS

Two Ways of Life Meet

By

HAROLD E. FEY AND D'ARCY McNICKLE

HARPER & BROTHERS   PUBLISHERS   NEW YORK

INDIANS AND OTHER AMERICANS

Copyright © 1959 by Harold E. Fey and D'Arcy McNickle

Library of Congress catalog card number: 58–10368

ACKNOWLEDGMENTS

RARELY is an idea entirely new. Men have trod the ground before, however thick the undergrowth may seem. In the field of Indian affairs, with its many obscure bypaths leading nowhere, men have made clearings and built monuments.

Much of what is said or suggested in *Indians and Other Americans* has been said or suggested by others; not always in written form. The men and women working in the field, as government clerks or mission station functionaries, the Indians themselves, are the original sources. The authors are first of all indebted to many such unnamed teachers and students.

We also warmly acknowledge our gratitude to the National Congress of American Indians, and to Mrs. Helen Peterson, its executive secretary, for counsel and assistance.

Of a more formal nature are our debts of gratitude to the authors and publishers whose works we have consulted in our search for data. Permission to quote from published material was courteously extended by the following:

Oxford University Press for the quotation from Arnold J. Toynbee's *A Study of History*, Abridgment of Volumes I–VI by D. C. Somervell, 1947.

The Yale Law Journal for the quotation from "The Erosion of Indian Rights" by Felix S. Cohen, Vol. 62, No. 3, 1953.

Dr. Sol Tax for material taken from the paper presented before the 1956 meeting of the American Anthropological Association evaluating Indian population figures; for the material quoted from the "Symposium" on The Fox Project, 1956; and for the statements on urban relocation of Indians which appeared originally as a mimeographed research proposal.

University of Oklahoma Press for the material from *Elias*

5

Boudinot, Cherokee, and His America by Ralph Henry Gabriel, 1941.

Dr. Gordon Macgregor for the quotation from *Warriors without Weapons*, University of Chicago Press, 1946.

The Johns Hopkins Press for the material quoted from *The Savages of America* by Roy Harvey Pearce, 1953.

The Brookings Institution for the quotations taken from *The Problem of Indian Administration* by Lewis Meriam and Associates, 1928.

Alfred A. Knopf for the quotations from *Progress and Power* by Carl L. Becker, 1936.

Columbia University Press, for the quotation from *The Idea of Progress in America, 1850–1860* by Arthur A. Ekirch, 1944.

University of South Carolina Press for the material appearing in *Indians of the South Carolina Frontier—the Edmund Atkin Report and Plan of 1755* by Wilbur R. Jacobs, 1954.

The *Annals* of the American Academy of Political and Social Science, for the quotation taken from "Recognition of Cultural Diversities in the Postwar World" by Ruth Benedict, July, 1943.

The Association on American Indian Affairs, Inc., for material quoted from several issues of *The American Indian*, and from the *Newsletter* of the Association for January, 1957.

The Bobbs-Merrill Company, Inc., for the quotation from *Mission for Peace* by William E. Warne, 1956.

CONTENTS

	ACKNOWLEDGMENTS	5
I.	A PREVIEW	13
II.	IN THE ORDER OF THEIR APPEARANCE	17
III.	HAUNTED BY HISTORY	25
IV.	CIVILIZATION EMBRACES THE INDIAN	32
V.	DEATH IN THE FIELD	38
VI.	GOVERNMENT BY CONSENT	47
VII.	MORALITY WITHIN LIMITS	57
VIII.	THE DEVELOPING DILEMMA	61
IX.	THE BANKRUPTCY OF GREAT EXPECTATIONS	70
X.	MEASURING RESULTS	80
XI.	REDEEMING THE PAST	91
XII.	EDUCATION FOR WHAT?	107
XIII.	DESTROYING THE FUTURE: (A) OPENING PHASE	120
XIV.	DESTROYING THE FUTURE: (B) FULL-SCALE ATTACK	129
XV.	LAW AS THE SOLVENT	138
XVI.	THE DISPOSSESSED	148
XVII.	THE SENSE OF CONGRESS	158
XVIII.	THE LONG VIEW	174
XIX.	UNFINISHED TASK	189
	MAP: DISTRIBUTION OF INDIAN LANGUAGE GROUPS	202
	APPENDIX	203
	NOTES	207
	INDEX	215

. . . When we Westerners call people "natives" we implicitly take the cultural colour out of our perception of them. We see them as wild animals infesting the country in which we happen to come across them, as part of the local flora and fauna and not as men of like passions with ourselves. So long as we think of them as "natives" we may exterminate them or, as is more likely today, domesticate them and honestly (perhaps not altogether mistakenly) believe that we are improving the breed, but we do not begin to understand them.

Arnold J. Toynbee: *A Study of History*

It is a pity that so many Americans today think of the Indian as a romantic or comic figure in American history without contemporary significance. . . . Like the miner's canary, the Indian marks the shifts from fresh air to poison gas in our political atmosphere; and our treatment of Indians, even more than our treatment of other minorities, reflects the rise and fall in our democratic faith.

Felix S. Cohen: *The Erosion of
Indian Rights, 1950–53*

INDIANS

AND

OTHER AMERICANS

I

A PREVIEW

This is a book about promises: some that were never uttered but filled the air, some uttered and broken, and some that remain as a dream to be fulfilled.

It is a book about people—about Indians. And therefore it is a book about change; how change is resisted and how, at times, it is accepted. In this matter of change, people are like the grass. They toss and sway and even seem to flow before the forces that make for change, as grass bows to the wind. But when the rude force moves on, people are found still rooted in the soil of the past. Again, like grass, people produce seed; and the seed will fly with the wind and, finding a friendly soil and climate, start a new generation. To change, yet to remain steadfast—that would seem to be the need of all living things.

The Indian people of the United States demonstrate such a need. This book will describe some of the ways in which change and resistance have worked in the lives of individuals and in tribal groups. To describe such processes should contribute to understanding, and would be reason enough for a book about Indians—but there are other strong reasons.

A commissioner of Indian affairs of fifty years ago, Francis E. Leupp,[1] made a discovery which deserves to be recorded here. As a public official often vexed by a badly informed public, the episode doubtless brought a certain gleam to his eye. Who knows how often that gleam may have reappeared in the eyes of Mr. Leupp's successors!

The incident described by Commissioner Leupp had its begin-

13

ning in a report unanimously adopted in 1909 at a gathering of representatives of several missionary boards working in the Indian country. The meeting concluded that "the sun dance and certain other Indian dances are essentially immoral in their tendency," and it was resolved "that the Department of Indian Affairs be requested to take more urgent steps to enforce their prohibition."

Mr. Leupp promptly wrote to each member attending the meeting and posed two questions: (1) In what way had the measures then in force failed in their objective of suppressing Indian dances? (2) What alternative or additional measures should be adopted for the purpose?

Leupp reported: "Every voter for the memorial assured me (1) That he did not know what methods I was already pursuing and (2) That he knew so little personally about the subject that he was unable to offer any advice." He concludes, and the gleam is certainly in his eye as he writes: "I refer to the incident, not for the purpose of being critical in turn, but to show how easily a body of men of pure character, high ideals and educated intelligence may be led into saying and doing the conventional thing in connection with Indian affairs, without a fraction of the mature consideration which they would feel obliged to give to almost any other of the government's manifold activities before passing judgment on its conduct."

To be knowledgeable about Indian affairs is not a mark of distinction in most social groups. Knowing the top ten batting averages in the two major baseball leagues might be a more valuable conversational asset.

Yet from time to time Indians get into the news columns. The Ute Indians win a $32,000,000 judgment award from the United States. The Klamath Indians of Oregon are legislated into disposing of one of the most valuable pine forests in the Pacific Northwest. The Pima hero of Iwo Jima destroys himself with white man's alcohol. Indians are relocated into our industrial cities, and become the subject of civic discussions.

We find ourselves talking about what ought to be done, possibly even writing letters to congressmen. We take a stand. Some of us begin to wish we knew more about the subject. We find ourselves in the position of Commissioner Leupp's memorialists.

Americans have an uneasy awareness of the red brother. The stories about him suggest that the white man in his contact with the Indian was often greedy, sometimes cruel, frequently insolent. The civilized man come to bring light into a somber primitive world has seemed himself to pass into shadow and become a doer of dark deeds.

This is what makes for uneasiness. Perhaps we can excuse the past—at least, today we are not responsible for it—if we can pull the pieces together and make the Indian story a success story.

And therein awaits a trap for the unwary. In recent years leading newspaper columnists have referred to Indian reservations as concentration camps and have urged their abolition. Politicians have made speeches about "emancipating" the Indians, making them "first class" citizens. Congress in 1953 laid down its own guiding policy, which is that "at the earliest possible time" the Indians of certain tribes and eventually all Indians in the United States "should be freed from federal supervision and control and from all disabilities and limitations especially applicable to Indians."[2]

Statements and proposals such as these are a recognition of the bad practices of the past; but they would wipe out the past by destroying the future for the Indian people.

To explain this apparent paradox, and to make clear the issues involved in this Indian situation, is the burden of this book.

In our American way, to understand is to want to do something. It is not our purpose to write an argument for a particular course of action, but rather to suggest a point of view out of which action may grow. The recommendations we will make in the end will reflect that point of view, and may be accepted or rejected on their merit.

But to have understanding is a first consideration. The facts are all about us; we need to pull them together, sort them out, and try to answer these natural questions: Who are the Indians and what is their status in contemporary American society? What happened to them after discovery and settlement by Europeans? How has the United States tried to help these firstcomers, and what is now being attempted in this line? Why has failure so clouded the record of government-Indian relations?

Other questions might be explored; however, these seem to encompass the essential details.

II

IN THE ORDER OF THEIR APPEARANCE

When Columbus reached the Western Hemisphere, an estimated 900,000 Indians lived in the territory that is now the United States.[1] This is an "educated" guess since contact with the Indian people was not made all at one time—a few groups were not reached until the middle of the nineteenth century. In some cases, when first contact was made, tribes that might have been numerous were greatly reduced in numbers. Plagues and wars resulting from tribal displacement had preceded the first white men. Our figure of 900,000 therefore represents a careful searching of the journals and reports of explorers, traders, religious missionaries, and official commissions of varying degrees of veracity.

We read accounts of how, when men first enter a long sealed tomb and admit the outside air, objects shatter before they are touched. The sudden change in atmospheric pressure breaks the static equilibrium and things fall apart. Something of the sort happened to the aboriginal populations in the Americas following the first entry of Europeans. The Pilgrim fathers landing on the Massachusetts coast found what seemed to be an empty and deserted land, though they could discern fields that had been planted to corn within the recent past. Later they were told that a plague (possibly scarlet fever) had destroyed the people in great numbers, and the Englishmen realized that the New England Indians had already been in contact with Europeans. This was not an isolated incident. Diseases which to Europeans seemed minor because they had developed resistances to them swept through Indian populations like fire in a pine forest. So severe

was the population decline that by 1880, if census counts are to
be relied upon, the Indians numbered about 250,000. Out of this
shadow of threatened racial extinction was fashioned the phrase
"vanishing Red Man."

Questions involving the Indian people, whether the questions
have to do with their legal status, their resources, or their aspirations, are surprisingly complex. And it is this complexity which
discourages friendly interest. Also it explains why programs
undertaken for the improvement of the Indian population often
fall short of the objective, and may in fact work a contrary result.

It should be possible, one would think, to arrive at a reasonably
accurate population count for the Indians; but one is quickly dis-
abused of this notion upon reading in a pamphlet issued by the
Bureau of Indian Affairs, *Resident Populations on Indian Reservations, 1950,* this comment: "Because there is no standard or universally accepted definition of the term Indian in the United
States law or usage, estimates of the total Indian population of
the country for 1950 or any other specific year necessarily will
vary in accordance with the definition being used." The extent of
the variance is then illustrated by the estimates released by the
Bureau of Census in 1950 and those released in the same year by
the Bureau of Indian Affairs. The Census Bureau counted 343,410
Indians, the Bureau of Indian Affairs, 368,401. Each bureau was
trying to count Indians. Moreover, in that particular year the two
bureaus worked closely together trying to arrive at a common,
workable definition. The schedule used by Census Bureau enu-
merators required the enumerator to ask the person being interviewed to identify himself by race, and most interviewers were
wary of asking the question. When working in a community predominantly Caucasian, the common practice was to place a check
mark after the word "white" unless the individual bore marked
characteristics of another race.

Accurate demographic data are extremely difficult to obtain.
Some Indians still live in primitive roadless areas, and many an
enumerator satisfies the demands of his job by inquiring at a convenient trading post for the names and ages of families in the
neighborhood. The fact that the same individual Indian may be

known under a variety of names—one on the official tribal census, one on the school enrollment, one attached to an allotment roll, the one he is currently using—adds a further hazard.

A critical analysis of material relating to the number and distribution of North American Indians is currently being pursued by Professor Sol Tax and associates in the Department of Anthropology at the University of Chicago.[2] The figures released by Professor Tax thus far are still tentative, but are more revealing than the figures of either the Bureau of Census or the Bureau of Indian Affairs. His total for 1950 is 571,824—a figure which he maintains is conservative. His estimate is important because it is based on a realistic definition and methodology. According to Professor Tax, "We count only Indians living in communities of Indians; but within those communities count only those who identify as Indians. And we have not counted important numbers of Indians who identify as Indians but not as part of such communities; we have not counted many communities of Indians such as the unenrolled Mississippi Choctaw in north Texas, Seminole in south Texas, and Catawba in Oklahoma and Arkansas. Nor have we counted fourteen groups in the southeast who are mixed Indian but think of themselves as new nationalities, and number some 10,000 people."

Of the nearly 572,000 Indians identified, Professor Tax concludes, almost 434,000 are "societal" Indians; that is, they are Indians who associate principally with other Indians in tribal communities, settlements, or reservations. In 1910, the Bureau of Indian Affairs estimated that there were 236,000 Indians who might fall within this definition; that is, they resided in and considered themselves part of tribal communities, settlements, or reservations. If this Bureau figure can be accepted as accurate (and probably it was a minimum figure), then in forty years Indians in this category have increased nearly 80 per cent. Professor Tax concludes: "Thus we cannot even say that while the number of Indians is increasing they are simply whites who still identify as Indians. Indians living in societies of Indians are increasing greatly in number."

Numbers by themselves do not convey the scope of Indian sur-

vival. Of the estimated 300 Indian languages spoken in the area
north of Mexico at the time of discovery, at least half are currently
in use. Kinship systems and lines of descent still function, often
at variance with government record systems and legal procedures. Individual Indians who dress and speak and act like any
contemporary American still play ordained roles as clansmen, as
members or even as heads of ritualistic societies, and as upholders
of a social order.

It is not out of any obstinate refusal to come to terms with
modern society that Indians oppose efforts, however well intended, to cut them away from their past. The reservations are
their homes, and Indians have the same attachment to the homeland as a Frenchman has to the sacred soil of France, or a Ger-
man to the Fatherland. This is understandable. For the same
reason they wish to retain their tribal organization, since this is
the manner by which their existence is formalized. In short,
Indian tribes are no more prepared to legislate themselves out of
existence, they are no more ready for annihilation, than is any
other group of people sharing a common history, a common language, and a system of commonly accepted goals in life.

The occupation of the so-called New World by Indian people
is ancient, the details of which are not generally known; even
less is known of the contributions of the Indian people to the
world's wealth. A brief review of some of these factors will help
to explain the Indian situation of today.

The story of the peopling of the Western Hemisphere by primitive men, possessed of the simplest of tools and weapons, is one of
the remarkable stories of human enterprise. The story is not a
connected one; many of the essential facts and time sequences are
missing. Inference and conjecture are often the only tools at hand
for recovering this buried past. Even so, the bold outlines of
man's achievements in the two continents are discernible.

Traveling on foot, without beasts of burden or wheeled
vehicles, groups of men, their womenfolk, their children, their
half-domesticated dogs, reached into every geographical region
and every climatic zone and established human settlement. Essentially they were physically all the same people, though the

accommodations they were required to make in spreading themselves from arctic tundra to tropic jungle developed societies that contrasted greatly one from another. There is no "Indian language," no "Indian religion," no "Indian character"—even the racial strain was a mixture of several physical types.

The time would come when the Indian people would be described as "more brutish than the beasts they hunt, more wild and unmanly than that unmanned wild country, which they range rather than inhabit."[3] Closer acquaintance with the record of occupation reveals that these people not only accommodated their bodies to extremes of temperature and climate but, again with the crudest of tools, caused a not always friendly environment to yield to their needs: they quarried rock to erect both individual houses and great community buildings; they diverted water to reclaim desert lands; they mined and processed the softer ores—gold, silver, and copper; they moved millions of cubic yards of earth to form bases for temples and public buildings in the Mississippi Valley; they were by all odds the greatest domesticators of food and fiber plants in the early history of man. They developed systems of mathematics which permitted a surprisingly accurate knowledge of the movement of the earth in its firmament. They were men of inquiring minds, a true segment of the human race.

The time span of these occurrences is one of the main fields of conjecture.

The evidence of the buried past—of fossilized bones and manmade tools of stone and bone—makes a strong case for supposing that men first came into the hemisphere some 20,000 or 25,000 years ago.[4] An even earlier date may eventually be accepted, but the probabilities are against that at the moment. At the time man may have been moving into what we have come to call the New World, sheets of ice closed and opened across the northern half of North America like great gates. Men would have had to slip in at a time when the gates were open—and the question of when will eventually be resolved by determining during which of three such openings migration occurred.

Speculation about the place of origin of man in the New World has quieted down. About every possible explanation has been offered at one time or another—a lost tribe of Israel, a tribe out of ancient Wales, children of the lost Atlantis, descendants of Egyptian sun worshipers; and it has even been strongly argued that the Indians are the autochthonous creation of the New World. The supposed resemblances to other peoples in other parts of the world were based usually on supposed resemblances of language, physical appearance, or religious beliefs and practices. None of these similarities stood up under close scrutiny. The case for a separate and independent evolution of a human stock in the Western Hemisphere must explain how it could happen that such development took place in the absence of prehominid life forms.

These speculations no longer hold our attention, in view of the growing body of archaeological findings. The case for the Asiatic origin of the American Indian via Bering Strait is by now reasonably well established—though no chronicler stood at Cape Prince of Wales to watch the first arrival.

The earliest migrating people seemed to have been distinguished by long-headedness (i.e., the ratio between a line drawn from front to back of the head and one drawn between the ears), though the recovery of skeletal material has been so scant for the very early period that any generalization must be tentative. By the time agriculture began to be practiced, the predominant physical type was broad-headed. The only point in mentioning such details is to suggest that migrating waves entered the New World over a time span of several thousands of years, and the earliest arrivals, going in advance of later waves, scattered in a variety of locations over a vast expanse of territory.

The evidence of language suggests such a development. The Hokan-Siouan language class contains the greatest number of separate linguistic families and individual languages, and the geographic spread of these languages extended from the Gulf of St. Lawrence (Iroquois) to California (Karok), and from the Canadian border (Assiniboine) to the Gulf of Mexico (Chitimacha). Not that this vast territory contained only this language type, but rather that large and small blocks of languages belonging in the type were scattered through the territory. The suggestion here is that segmentation and differentiation of language took place over a rather long period of time; also that considerable time lapses were involved in the movement of people to all the corners of the area described. Hence the assumption that the Hokan-Siouan speaking peoples may have been the first to migrate from the Asiatic world.

The reverse situation is presented by the Eskimo-Aleut people, who were probably the latest to arrive in the New World. They occupy the circumpolar land regions without interruption, and the language spoken from Greenland to the Aleutian Islands is essentially identical.

Of the other four great language groups (of Sapir's classification), the Penutian probably followed after the Hokan-Siouan, then Algonquian-Wakashan, Uto-Aztecan-Tanoan, and Na-dene. (See Appendix.)

The distribution of this aboriginal population is particularly interesting since it shows some marked contrasts with population densities in modern times. The greatest concentration of population prior to discovery seems to have occurred along the Pacific coast, with 43.3 inhabitants per 100 sq. km. for California and 28.3 for the Northwest coast extending into modern Alaska. This was predominantly a region in which fishing supplied livelihood, although in California an important supplementary food was derived from processing acorns to make a bread food.

The southwestern United States, which today is one of the least densely settled of all areas, in aboriginal times ranked just after the Northwest coast with 10.7 inhabitants per 100 sq. km. The climate of five hundred years ago was probably somewhat more favorable than it is today and the people were primarily agriculturists.

The eastern area, by which term is comprised the entire region east of the Mississippi River and all of the Atlantic coast, while supporting the greatest total number, had a relatively low density of 6.95 per 100 sq. km. A region as environmentally hostile as the Arctic coast, with 4.02 inhabitants per 100 sq. km., provided almost as much livelihood as the friendlier eastern region.

It may have seemed to the European colonizers that the land

was empty and poorly used or not used at all. We know today that this was not the case. Indians made quite adequate use of the land and resources, considering the tools and knowledge available to them; and in fact, culture techniques developed by the Indians for their native plants were adopted by the Europeans. The southwestern Indian who plants his corn and melons in a pile of sand is utilizing technical skills which no school of agriculture could improve upon. Techniques for surviving in the Arctic were copied from the Eskimo people and taught to armed forces personnel in World War II.

III

HAUNTED BY HISTORY

WHEN Europeans and Indians met for the first time in the Western Hemisphere 450 years ago, neither side was prepared for the event. The Europeans were looking for quite a different land —a land of spices, shimmering silks, and dancing girls. The Indies! And quite naturally, Columbus and his followers insisted that indeed this was what they had found. The Indians, for their part, had no expectations and were hopeful at first that the strange creatures would go away.

The thousands of years of history experienced by the peoples who had lived for so long on opposite sides of the Atlantic Ocean made for quite different outlooks, vastly different material culture; they prepared the one for victory, the other for vanquishment. The European experience had developed in men aggressive, outgoing energy. It had encouraged in them an unquestioning faith in their destiny, a belief in the invincibility of their institutions and systems. Along with this had been developed machines for war and for domestic uses which made it possible to support the good opinions they had of themselves.

The Indian experience seemed to make men who had a craving for anonymity—the quality that President Franklin Roosevelt looked for in his White House assistants. Some aboriginal groups developed a hunger for territory and encroached upon their neighbors. The record is not clear, but it is possible that their conquest of territory was incidental to prosecution of a game called war. However it was, ideologies were not a part of it. Indians did not go forth to plant the "true faith" in infidel lands.

And material culture, while it had many subtleties and often reflected a high order of thinking in the realm of the natural sciences—particularly as it developed plant domestication and herbalism and explored mathematical laws—did not run to mechanical invention and production.

The attribute in which the two races stood farthest apart was in the knowledge and practice of writing. A rudimentary form of writing had appeared in Middle America, but it had not become a common possession. Already the notion was gaining ground, at least in Europe, that literacy was the true mark of civilized man. The Indian people, without a written language, were rated by early settlers as little better than the beasts of the forest. Europeans of impeccable moral behavior counted it no blotch upon their record to use their skill in writing to double-deal and overreach the Indians. There were notable exceptions, in men like William Penn, Roger Williams, and the Calverts of Maryland.

The prime source of misunderstanding between these representatives of two traditions resulted from their quite different attitudes toward land.[1] To the European, land was merchantable. Law and usage had developed a complicated system of privileges and obligations, all deriving from the notion of a transferable fee title in land. Land that was not encompassed within some form of recorded title was outside of law itself—something as anomalous as a person beyond the pale of any country. When these Europeans found that Indians had no proceedings for recording title, indeed had no titles, they readily assumed that there was no ownership. They were beasts that ranged the land rather than occupied it.

Property is a function of any society. If the European settlers had been able to get at the facts, and had been interested in the facts, they would have found that surface areas were recognized, boundaries were respected, use rights were sustained. But nothing in Indian practices required that land be divided up and parceled out under any system of titles.

In practice this meant that tribes knew their own territory, as they knew their neighbors', and unless they were bent on mischief they stayed within their own bounds. It also meant that within the domain of any given tribe, subordinate-use rights were recognized in separate bands, in clans, and even in family groups. Among the hunting tribes which commonly were thought of as moving indiscriminately over trackless wastes, there were well-defined hunting territories, each claimed and used by an identifiable group. After fur trapping became a principal source of livelihood among the northern tribes, a system of individual property rights developed. But here, as in all matters touching on land, the right was a right to use, not to transfer in the market place.[2]

This Indian system would be explained and defended many years later (in 1881), at a time when Congress was considering a bill to compel Indian tribes to divide their land holdings among their individual members. The so-called Five Civilized Tribes (the tribes which at that time had advanced farthest in adopting white men's practices) petitioned the Congress to allow them to continue their own system. The petition, offered in despair, recited these facts: "Our people have not asked for or authorized this, for the reason that they believe it could do no good and would only result in mischief in their present condition. Our own laws regulate the system of land tenure suited to our condition, and much safer than that which is proposed for it.

"Improvements can be and frequently are sold, but the land itself is not a chattel. Its occupancy and possession are indispensable to holding it, and its abandonment for two years makes it revert to the public domain. In this way every one of our citizens is assured of a home. The change to individual title would throw the whole domain in a few years into the hands of a few persons."

The petition concluded on a practical note: "A large portion of our country, and at least two-thirds of the Indian country, are only suitable for grazing purposes. No man can afford to live by stock raising and herding who is restricted to 160 or even 320 acres, especially on lands away from water."[3]

The Europeans of good faith, the William Penns and Lord Calverts, pursued honorable courses by European standards. In fact, they went considerably beyond the common practice of their day in offering compensation for the lands they desired to possess. But even where the action was taken in good will, it is doubtful whether the Indians understood the nature of the transaction or could have agreed to it if they had understood. The accepting of gifts and the giving of gifts in return was something they understood. Or inviting a stranger to come into one's house and share one's food, that too was understood and universally practiced. But giving the right of permanent possession of the soil under one's feet—that was not part of the social scheme.

In time to come, Indians would learn to negotiate and to bargain, to exact as high a price as they could for what the white man wanted, but they never reconciled themselves to the idea. Even today, when Indian tribes may go into court and sue the United States for inadequate compensation or no compensation for lands taken from them, they still are dealing in alien concepts. One cannot grow a tree on a pile of money, or cause water to gush from it; one can only spend it, and then one is homeless.

The nature of land tenure was not understood—or more properly, it should be said that Europeans understood it in the way they wanted it to be. It was essential to them that they have title, a document which could be made of record, sold, and handed on to successors.

The United States Supreme Court in time gave full recognition to this need and the processes that resulted from it. John Marshall's sonorous opinion of the matter was stated in 1823.[4] Worth noting here is the passage: "While the different nations of Europe respected the right of the native, as occupants, they asserted the ultimate dominion to be in themselves; and claimed and exercised, as a consequence of this ultimate dominion, a power to grant the soil, while yet in possession of the natives. These grants have been understood by all, to convey a title to the grantees, subject only to the Indian right of occupancy."

The opinion further recognized that it was concerned with a practical situation, not with the morality of the situation. It continued:

However extravagant the pretension of converting the discovery of an inhabited country into conquest may appear; if the principle has been asserted in the first instance, and afterwards sustained; if the country has been acquired and held under it; if the property of the great mass of the community originates in it, it becomes a law of the land, and cannot be questioned. However this restriction may be opposed to natural right, and to the usages of civilized nations, yet, if it be indispensable to that system under which the country has been settled, and be adapted to the actual condition of the two people, it may, perhaps, be supported by reason, and certainly cannot be rejected by courts of justice.

In its practical application, the doctrine recognized and confirmed the procedures set up by the incoming Europeans; but it also created ex post facto guarantees that the Indians could not be denied due process. Later we shall see how this doctrine has worked out as a protection to the Indian people.

The Europeans brought with them still another concept about land which widely affected Indian occupancy of their own shores. This had to do with the uses to which lands are put.

Even though Englishmen in their first landings might search out and raid Indian storehouses of corn and dried vegetables and be saved from starvation by gifts of Indian produce, still they persisted in calling Indians roaming hunters. And hunters they were, on that eastern seaboard and far inland.

They were farmers also, and this the Englishmen also knew. Indians had brought corn, the semitropical grass, into a state of domestication so complete that, unlike other cereals, it must rely on man's nurturing hand for propagation. A head of wheat or barley, on ripening, will blow with the wind and reseed itself. The wild grass out of which corn originated probably had a winged seed which was wind-borne. But in modern corn the ear falls to the ground, its kernels all sprout, and none can mature because they rob each other of food and moisture. The Indian people, moreover, had acclimatized the plant from the humid lowland of its origin to extremes of temperature and soil and moisture conditions.[5]

The people who accomplished this horticultural feat could not have spent their time idly roaming. There are areas in the southwestern United States where for at least 4,000 years the Indians had subsisted entirely as agriculturists. In the remains of their habitations one finds grinding stones and digging tools almost to the exclusion of projectile points.

But so long as Europeans could think of the Indians as unseated hunters, they could justify to their own consciences the assertion that as civilized men they had a higher claim upon the land—a view supported by Vattel, one of the first writers on international law, in his *Law of Nations* (1758).

In one notable case this doctrine of superior use endowing civilized man with superior rights was tested, and found to be not so much a moral doctrine as a subterfuge.

The testing agent was the Cherokee tribe, which, beginning about 1790, set out to become civilized.[6] Aided by missionary workers, and provided with material help under the terms of a treaty with the United States by which in exchange for land they received farming tools, spinning wheels, looms, and other implements, the Cherokees began to remake their lives in the image of the white man. Some years later, in 1826, a full-blooded member of that tribe, bearing the name of the New Jersey philanthropist Elias Boudinot, was able to stand up before the First Presbyterian Church in Philadelphia and report on the progress of his people: "It is a matter of surprise to me, and must be to all those who are properly acquainted with the condition of the aborigines of the country, that the Cherokees have advanced so far and so rapidly in civilization. . . . At this time there are 22,000 cattle; 7,600 horses; 46,000 swine; 2,500 sheep; 762 looms; 1,488 spinning wheels; 172 wagons; 2,948 plows; 10 saw mills; 31 grist mills; 62 blacksmith shops; 8 cotton machines; 18 schools; 18 ferries; and a number of public roads. In one district there were, last winter, upward of 1,000 volumes of good books."

Only a few years before, in 1821, Sequoya had invented the Cherokee alphabet, and Boudinot became the first editor of the *Cherokee Phoenix*, printed in Sequoya's script. In 1827 the people adopted a written constitution, providing for an executive, a bicameral legislature, a supreme court, and a code of laws.

This the Cherokees accomplished in a single lifetime, with the deliberate purpose in mind of being allowed to remain, as members of a civilized society, in the homeland they had always known in the mountain country where Georgia, Tennessee, and North Carolina come together.

They even carried to the United States Supreme Court their plea for recognition as a self-governing people. They won their case—the Court upheld their plea as against the presumption of the state of Georgia in extending its law over Cherokee territory —but victory in the Court could not save the Cherokees. Civilization was not necessarily a formula to protect human rights. It was a question of whose rights were involved.

President Jackson refused to honor the court's decision. "John Marshall has made his decision; let him enforce it," was the President's response. The Congress, at Jackson's insistence, had already adopted the Indian Removal Act of 1830. The Cherokees and all the tribes of the Southeast and the old Northwest were required to move to the wilderness west of the Mississippi River. When they resisted, the government countered with armed force. Thus they yielded to the usages of civilization.

It mattered not that Senator Frelinghuysen of New Jersey declaimed in the Senate chamber: "God, in His providence, planted these tribes on this western continent, so far as we know, before Great Britain herself had a political existence. I believe, sir, it is not now seriously denied that the Indians are men, endowed with kindred faculties and powers with ourselves. . . . In the light of natural law, can a reason for a distinction exist in the mode of enjoying that which is my own? If I use it for hunting, may another take it because he needs it for agriculture? . . . Is it one of the prerogatives of the white man, that he may disregard the dictates of moral principles, when an Indian shall be concerned?"[7]

The Senator was answered by the fact.

IV

CIVILIZATION EMBRACES THE INDIAN

TAKEN by themselves, certain events in the long history of Indian-white relations in the New World have a shocking impact on sensibility. By themselves, the events suggest that they could only have been the acts of wicked and depraved men. Yet seen in different circumstances, the same men—an Andrew Jackson, or the Georgians who prosecuted Samuel Worcester, the missionary to the Cherokee Indians—were law-abiding, home-loving, even men of heroic stature.

Obviously, it is necessary to look for understanding behind the events. Some recent writers, and some older, have examined this long Indian record and have arrived at observations which, while they are not edifying, help to explain the record.

The explanation rests at least in part on the nature of the society which produced western European man—if the use of such a symbol will be allowed.

Carl L. Becker, the historian, has described in illuminating detail the development of this society.[1]

The point of differentiation of the European from earlier human experience begins, in Becker's analysis, when men gave up mere verbal manipulation of ideas, magical or otherwise, and became involved in the manipulation of things. "Whereas other peoples—the Hindus and the Chinese and the Hellenized peoples of western Asia—remained relatively immobile, fixed within the places where they had long dwelt, content with repeating the activities and adhering to the ideas that use and custom make familiar, the Europeans alone are always on the move, pushing beyond their frontiers, spreading themselves ever more dominantly over the habitable globe."

This kind of racial adventuring produced men who grew increasingly practical, increasingly cocksure of themselves. Soon they saw themselves as a chosen people—everything worked for them. From this assurance they could look down upon the static peoples of the world (and the Indians would fall into that category) and call them infidels. When they reached that point, they were ready to march upon and conquer the world.

Becker pursues the analysis: "Starting out as defenders of the Christian faith, they gradually lose interest in the Holy City and look for more tangible utopias: compromising with the infidels in return for their fabrics and treasure, they become increasingly preoccupied with the outer world of things and with the implements essential to the appropriation of its material advantages. The social manifestation of this preoccupation is the increase in numbers and in power of the burgher class, which imperceptibly, unconsciously, imposes its mental temper on the European mind."

The logical development moves on: "Thus there emerges, within the European climate of opinion, and as a rationalization of the practical interests of a burgher society, the idea of human Progress. . . . Of all the inventions yet made by the ingenious Europeans, the doctrine of progress is the most effective, the most revolutionary and dislocating, since it transforms a Deo-centric into a Homo-centric universe, and thereby makes man the measure of all things."

Until at last logic falters: "Never before have men made relatively greater progress in the rational control of physical force, or relatively less in the rational control of social relations. . . . The forces of nature have been discovered and applied by a few exceptional individuals, whereas every effort to ameliorate human relations has been frustrated by the fact that society cannot be transformed without the compliance of the untutored masses."

It is this logical and inevitable extension of the European experience as a force in the world which is disturbing to contemplate. It accounts for the events that befell the Indian people —and, equally, native peoples all over the world. Wherever Europeans went to colonize and to dig out the raw materials for their factories and mills, they carried the idea of progress with them, and people were impoverished.

Roy Harvey Pearce examines the history of Indian-White relations from a similar point of view.[2] He remarks on the fact that many of the first explorers and settlers in the New World found that the Indians possessed knowledge and skills of a high order. But later, when white men sought to push the Indian off the land he had occupied from time immemorial, he was discovered to be a stubborn obstacle to progress, an enemy of civilization.

Pearce writes: "Americans who were setting out to make a new society could find a place in it for the Indian only if he would become what they were—settled, steady, civilized. Yet somehow he would not be anything but what he was—roaming, unreliable, savage. So they concluded that they were destined to try to civilize him and, in trying, to destroy him, because he could not and would not be civilized."

He notes that even Lewis H. Morgan, sometimes called the father of American anthropology, gave respectability to the notion that Indians were incapable of growth. Admitting the fine qualities of integrity, generosity, unbounded hospitality, love of truth, and unshaken fidelity, Morgan concluded: "There was, however, a fatal deficiency in Indian society, in the non-existence of a progressive spirit. . . . There was neither progress, nor invention, nor increase of political wisdom. Old forms were preserved, old customs adhered to."

Arthur A. Ekirch, in the course of studying American society of the early nineteenth century, reports how in public statements by political leaders and in press and magazine articles the idea of the superior rights of civilized men was given currency.[3] A writer for the *Southern Review* observed (1828): "We can perceive neither justice, nor wisdom, nor humanity, in arresting the progress of order and science, that unproductive and barren wastes may be reserved for the roaming barbarian."

A contemporary magazine, the *Western Monthly Review*, in the same year, carried an article which deplored the failure of the Indians to learn the white man's arts. Urging the abandonment of the reservation policy, this writer argued: "As separate and independent people, with communities of their own, they will always tend toward barbarism."

Helen Hunt Jackson investigated and wrote about some of the practical consequences of these attitudes.[4] Her book, A Century of Dishonor, is no longer fashionable. It was an accusatory book, hard-hitting and factual, much too good a book to be forgotten, though it makes for uncomfortable reading. The pioneering Bishop H. B. Whipple of Minnesota wrote an introduction, charging that "The American people have accepted as truth the teaching that the Indians were a degraded, brutal race of savages, who it was the will of God should perish at the approach of civilization. If they do not say with our Puritan fathers that these are the Hittites who are to be driven out before the saints of the Lord, they do accept the teaching that manifest destiny will drive the Indians from the earth. The inexorable has no tears or pity at the cries of anguish of the doomed race."

One of the events investigated by Helen Hunt Jackson was the Sand Creek massacre which took place in Colorado in 1864. The Civil War was on, and armed raiding parties were abroad. The governor of Colorado invited a camp of several hundred Cheyenne Indians to come into the neighborhood of the forts for protection, and the Cheyennes in accepting the invitation settled near Fort Lyon. Later they were asked to move to Sand Creek, about forty miles away, and were guaranteed safe conduct. Government rations were issued. About the time of the removal to Sand Creek, a wagon train was attacked some miles to the north and the Sand Creek Cheyennes were blamed for this. Without warning, the village was attacked by a force of Colorado cavalry and some United States soldiers, all under the command of Colonel J. M. Chivington.

A congressional committee which investigated the affair in 1868 concluded: "It scarcely had its parallel in the records of Indian barbarity. Fleeing women, holding up their hands and praying for mercy, were shot down; infants were killed and scalped in derision; men were tortured and mutilated. . . . A war ensued which cost the government $30,000,000 and carried conflagration and death into the border settlements. During the spring and summer of 1865 no less than 8,000 troups were withdrawn from the effective forces engaged in the rebellion to meet this Indian war."

Among the signers of this official report was Lieutenant General William T. Sherman.

The event at Sand Creek is far removed in time and place from the first faltering landings on the northeast coast, but the men and women who made the landings carried the seed which would come to fruit in good time. As human beings, they accepted the hospitality of the surprisingly friendly savages on the shore; but as Europeans they were doomed to destroy their own hosts.

Helen Hunt Jackson investigated the story of Old Crow, a Cheyenne chief who served as a scout under General Crook. He recited: "I did not feel like doing anything for a while because I had no heart. I did not want to be in this country. I was all the time wanting to get back to the better country where I was born, and where my children are buried, and where my mother and sister yet live. So I laid in my lodge most of the time with nothing to think about but that, and the affair up north at Fort Robinson, and my relatives and friends who were killed there. But now I feel as though if I had a wagon and horse or two and some land, I would try to work."

The affair "up north at Fort Robinson" which preyed so upon Old Crow's mind was described in a ruling of the Court of Claims in the case of *Connors* v. *U.S.*[5] After telling of the surrender of Dull Knife's band of northern Cheyennes and their deportation to Indian Territory, where most of their children died, the court said: "After a year of sickness, misery and bitterness in the Territory, and repeated prayers to be taken back to the country where their children could live, 320 of them in September of 1878 broke away from their reservation. Dull Knife and Little Wolf were the leaders. They were pursued and overtaken. A parley ensued in which Little Wolf, whom Captain Bourke characterizes as 'one of the bravest in fights where all were brave,' said 'We do not want to fight you, but we will not go back.' The troops instantly fired upon the Cheyennes and a new Indian war began."

The fighting reduced the Cheyenne numbers by half, but 148 were rounded up and carried as prisoners to Fort Robinson in Wyoming. The court continues its account:

There they persistently refused to return to the reservation and were kept in close custody. In January 1879 orders from the Interior Department arrived at Fort Robinson pre-emptorially directing the commanding officer to remove them to the reservation. . . . Their unequivocal answer was: "We will die, but we will not go back."

The commanding officer apparently shrank from shooting them down. . . . The military authorities therefore resorted to the means for subduing the Cheyennes by which a former generation of animal trainers subdued wild beasts. In the midst of the dreadful winter, with the thermometer 40° below zero, the Indians, including the women and children, were kept for five days and nights without food or fuel, and for three days without water. At the end of that time they broke out of the barracks, and rushed forth into the night. The troops pursued, firing upon them as upon enemies at war. . . . Twelve days later the pursuing cavalry came upon the remnant of the band in a ravine fifty miles from Fort Robinson. The troops encircled the Indians, leaving no possible avenue of escape. The Indians fired upon them, killing a lieutenant and two privates. The troops advanced. The Indians, then without ammunition, rushed in desperation toward the troops with hunting knives in hand; but before they had advanced many paces, a volley was discharged by the troops and all was over.

The final result of the last Cheyenne war was that, of the 320 who broke away in September, seven wounded Cheyennes were sent back to the reservation.

At this point the idea of progress had carried about as far as it could go in one direction.

V

DEATH IN THE FIELD

THE events described up to now have a remoteness in time which may seem to remove them from our concern. "Let the dead past bury the dead" might suggest itself as a suitable response to the unhappy record of the Indians.

However, the past never dies. The story that seems to come to an end against a wintry landscape in Wyoming turns out to be only one phase in a larger clash of events and purposes. Some episodes, having beginnings in the long ago, are still working their way to a conclusion and forcing us to recognize responsibilities and obligations—forcing us to act, if we can, to avert disasters still in the making.

Such a challenge is brought by the Pima Indians of Arizona.

When in 1534 Fray Marcos de Niza first entered the Pima country—Pima Alta, the Spanish writers called it—he found the Indians farming the land on both banks of the Gila River, diverting the river water with their brush and mud dams and bringing the water through hand-dug canals many miles through the flat valley land. What Fray Marcos could not have realized (only recent archaeological investigation has brought the record to light) was that the irrigation canals he saw in operation had their beginnings as early perhaps as 500 A.D. There is reason to believe, indeed, that the Pimans of today are descendants of the first people to practice agriculture in what is now the United States. At one location situated within the Papago reservation, archaeological excavation indicates a time span of 10,000 years. The earliest occupation was by people of the so-called Lake Cochise culture, people who had largely given up hunting and subsisted on wild fruits and seeds which they processed between grinding stones. How old agriculture is in the area is still to be finally determined. But at one location (Bat Cave), in a shallow valley lying just beyond the headwaters of the Gila River, maize has been recovered from deposits that are between 4,000 and 4,500 years old.[1]

When Fray Marcos visited the Pima Indians, hunting was with them largely a ceremonial occupation, except as small game might be brought in to provide some variety in diet. The people were farmers, and they were quick to recognize the value of the wheat and barley which Father Kino brought them many years later (1697), together with horses and cattle. Left largely to themselves, the Pimas planted their fields, stored their surpluses. In 1857, the San Antonio-San Diego stage line was established, and in that year the Pima Indians sold 100,000 pounds of wheat and quantities of vegetables to the proprietors. In 1859, the stage line purchased 250,000 pounds of wheat; and in 1860, 440,000 pounds.

In 1859, the United States established a reservation for the Pima Indians, confirming use rights in lands which the Pimas and their ancestors had used since before the beginning of the Christian era.[2] These rights had previously been confirmed by Spain, and later by Mexico, and the United States could hardly do less.

The special representative of the United States who visited the Pimas in that year reported: "There are some fine lands on the Gila and any extensive cultivation above the Indian fields will cause trouble about the water for irrigation and inevitably bring about a collision between the settlers and the Indians."

The warning was timely regarding the possible pre-emption of Gila River water, but it reflected unfairly on the peaceful habits of the Pima Indians. Never once in after years did the Pimas even threaten retaliation for what was taken from them.

The first permanent appropriation of Gila River water by a non-Indian occurred in 1868, though doubtless there were temporary diversions even before that time. So quickly did settlers pour into the upper Gila River valley after the Civil War that by 1871 the Commissioner of Indian Affairs reported to the Secretary of Interior: "People who have lived on the Gila for years tell me there never was before such a thing as a dry bed on this reserve at this time of year. . . . Our Indians are much dissatisfied and blame the settlers who are above us for taking their water." The government responded to appeals for help from the Indians in 1873 by making repairs to old Indian ditches, some of which went back to prehistoric times. Thereafter, for thirty years, government assistance consisted in paying the salary of ditch riders and minor maintenance costs.

By 1873, the settlers in the Safford Valley above the Pima Indians began the construction of community canals, large works, representing considerable investments of time and money. After about 1890, water no longer flowed in the lower Gila River except in the off season, when it was not needed for irrigation, and of course during periods of flood.

The first discussion about the advisability of building storage facilities to capture flood waters occurred in 1896, but these discussions only resulted in field investigations carried out by the United States Geological Survey, the United States Bureau of Reclamation, the Army Engineers, and the Bureau of Indian Affairs. The first attempt to supplement the Indian water supply was made in 1903–4, when five wells were dug at Sacaton, the Pima Agency. Between 1905 and 1906, eight additional wells were dug and a short canal and side ditches were constructed to divert flood waters. The system was designed to irrigate about 10,000 acres, although in prehistoric times the Indians had irrigated in excess of 25,000 acres.

Finally came the great event for which the Pima Indians had petitioned and their friends and professional advisers had pleaded for years. On June 7, 1924, Congress authorized the construction of the Coolidge Dam in the box canyon of the Gila River. Army Engineers had been directed in 1912 to conduct a study as to the feasibility of such construction, and finally the reports were all in, the site selected, and cost estimates checked and confirmed.

The language of the Coolidge Dam Act was specific as to the uses that would be made, and the priority of use, of the waters to be impounded. The language read: "For the purpose, *first*, of providing water for the irrigation of lands allotted to Pima Indians on the Gila River Reservation, Arizona, now without an adequate supply of water and, *second*, for the irrigation of such other lands in public or private ownership, as in the opinion of the Secretary [of the Interior], can be served *without diminishing the supply necessary for said Indian lands*," etc.[3]

That should have settled the matter. The Indians had first right to the river through immemorial use, and Congress in authorizing the Coolidge Dam construction recognized and confirmed these rights. But the matter was not so easily settled. A prior congressional act (June 30, 1917) had provided that water diverted from the Gila River should be distributed to the Indians and to private and public lands "in accordance with the respective rights and priorities of such lands," these rights and priorities to be determined by the Secretary of the Interior "or by a court of competent jurisdiction."

A determination had not been made, and therefore a suit was instituted for the purpose of adjudicating this question. Presumably the Indian lands and water rights should not have been included in the court review, since both the prior act and the Coolidge Dam Act treated the Indian lands as a class apart.

What exactly occurred in the court proceedings the Indians never knew. They were represented before the court by the solicitor for the Department of the Interior; and when they requested a private attorney to attend in their behalf, the attorney was barred from the room.

The determination of the court, entitled "Gila River Decree" (entered June 29, 1935), is a curious document, characterized by a later attorney for the Pima Indians as "one of the greatest crimes of water law." The court did not confine itself to a determination of the priorities of private and public lands, as the prior legislation directed should be done. Instead, the rights by immemorial use were commingled with rights of lesser priority, and all, Indian and white users, were found to be "entitled to share equally in all of the stored and pumped water" of the project.

Ordinarily, the law of the river is decided on a "first come, first served" basis. Priorities of use are strictly enforced against

later comers, and in the early days of the West a man enforced
his rights at rifle point, if necessary. The Indians could not, or
would not, use a gun. After all, their own legal protector had
represented them and signed in their name. It was the court and
the legal protector that brought about the anomalous result, not
the other water users.

The matter did not come to rest at that point.

In their early history, the Pimas had constructed their own
diversion dams, using brush and rocks and mud. The dams might
be washed away with each spring freshet, but were easily re-
placed at the start of the irrigation season. Their canals were hand
dug, followed the natural meanders of the land, and were easily
cleaned and kept in repair. After the construction of Coolidge
Dam, the Indian system was rebuilt by modern engineers. The
canals were greatly enlarged and involved the construction of
expensive siphons, drops, regulating gates, and pertinent struc-
tures. Ditch cleaning was no longer a hand-labor affair but required heavy and expensive power machinery.

It became necessary for the Pima Indians to pay an annual
assessment in cash in order to have water delivered to the land.
They had always been subsistence farmers, not producers for a
commercial market. Moreover, some years previously the government had divided up the Pima lands into ten-acre allotments
within the irrigable area and ten acres of nonirrigable land in the
surrounding desert. Plots of this size compelled the Indians to remain subsistence farmers and offered little hope that they would
ever be able to realize enough cash to pay their water assess-
ments.

When the Indians balked at paying operation and maintenance
costs, the government hit upon what was thought to be a happy
solution. At considerable expense it subjugated and brought under
the ditch a 10,000-acre plot of the desert land and proposed that
this land be leased out to non-Indian operators and the income
used to pay operation and maintenance costs on all the Pima
lands.

Pimas born after allotments were made, for whom no land was

available, yielded reluctantly before this decision. Landlessness would continue to be their lot.

In still another respect the Pima Indians were thwarted and brought to desperate measures by the men appointed to manage their affairs.

The Coolidge Dam Act provided that a landowner's agreement should be entered into between the Secretary of the Interior and water users to be benefited by the dam. By terms of the agreement subsequently entered into, all irrigation wells within the district were brought under and made part of the project. This was intended to guarantee that no water user would exceed the amount of water allotted to him by drilling wells which would divert from the underground channel of the Gila River. The design of the project was such, however, that water coming down from the dam was diverted first to the Indian lands. In order to provide water in equal amount to the non-Indian lands, the project drilled irrigation wells and pumped the water into the canals serving the non-Indian lands. The situation was further complicated by landowners residing outside of the project area who drilled wells, claiming that the underground water they were tapping was not the property of the irrigation project.

The dry years which succeeded the construction of Coolidge Dam upset all calculations and particularly the policy affecting the drilling of irrigation wells. The reduced flow in the river (storage behind the dam disappeared entirely in the driest of these years) resulted in wholly inadequate supplies of water for the growing of crops. Year after year Indian farmers failed to make a crop, wasting labor and seed as well. On the other hand, the wells drilled to supply the white-owned lands continued to pump water, even though the water table dropped at alarming rates during the dry years.

The Pimas, through actions of their tribal government and through their private attorney, implored the government to finance the drilling of wells to serve the Pima ditches. For whatever reason, the Bureau of Indian Affairs seemed unable to secure funds for the purpose. The Indians wondered whether political pressure exerted by the white water users was responsible, acting either upon the Department of the Interior or upon members of Congress.

Finally, toward the end of 1953, the Indians took matters into their own hands. Without official approval from the Department, they drilled four irrigation wells, using funds they had accumulated through cropping operations on tribal land. The cost of drilling a deep well and equipping it with the necessary pump and outlet may amount to anywhere from $10,000 to $25,000, so it was not a matter to be lightly undertaken.

When the wells were completed, fresh obstacles were encountered. The electric power to drive the pumps was supplied by a government line, and the Indians were denied power. The Secretary telegraphed an order that water from the wells was not to be used until the chief legal officer of the department could render an opinion as to whether the Indians were entitled to use the water under their own lands. By such devices, the Indians were prevented from using their wells from the summer of 1954 to the spring of 1955, the loss of a growing season. Then the order was relaxed.

It is now a hundred years since the United States established a reservation for the Pima Indians, presumably for the purpose of protecting their rights and advancing them in civilization. The net effect has been that today the Pima Indians are farming about one-half the acreage they had under cultivation a hundred years ago.

That is the gross aspect of the story. What happened to the inner life of the Pima people is more closely reflected in what happened to their son, Ira Hayes.

Many Americans will have heard of Ira Hayes, the Pima Indian who with his five mates in the Marine Corps raised the United States flag on Mount Suribachi on the island of Iwo Jima. He was in the photograph, now world-famous, taken by Joe Rosenthal. But Ira Hayes died of acute alcoholism in a cotton field on the Pima reservation on a night in January 1955. He lay all night on the cold ground, and death was attributed to "exposure." What had happened in the ten years intervening since the dramatic moment on Mount Suribachi?

On November 12, 1953, the *Arizona Republic*, the Phoenix morning newspaper, reported that Hayes spent the previous night in jail on a drunk-and-disorderly charge. The reporter did some digging in the files, and found that this was the forty-second occasion that Hayes had been arrested on such a charge. There would be still other arrests between November, 1953, and January, 1955.

He had served throughout the South Pacific, fighting at Vella Lavella and Bougainville before coming up to Iwo Jima, where he served for thirty-six days and came out unwounded. After the flag-raising incident he and two of his buddies were brought back to the United States to travel extensively in support of the seventh war loan. One of these buddies reported that Hayes refused to be leader of a platoon because, as he explained, "I'd have to tell other men to go and get killed, and I'd rather do it myself." He was reluctant to return home, but was given no choice. That started a round of speaking engagements, parades, ticker tape—and people offering hospitality. The hospitality, unfortunately, invariably included free liquor, and Ira drank greedily. It was the quickest way to blur the painful, heedless publicity to which he was subjected.

After his discharge he went home to Arizona, in the district called Bapchule. After the excitement of war and the hectic round of living which he had just experienced, Hayes' Indian home was not a place in which he could settle down at once. His was no longer a self-sufficient family, such as Hayes might have known in his own childhood, which certainly his ancestors had known before him. Without adequate water to grow crops, with land-holdings reduced beyond any hope of economic livelihood even if there had been water, it was not a place for a returning warrior to rest and mend. Too many other mouths depended on the food he would eat.

With the help of the relocation program of the Bureau of Indian Affairs, he went to Chicago and found employment with the International Harvester Company. For a while things went well with him, then he began drinking again. He was picked up on Skid Row in Chicago, dirty and shoeless, and sent to jail. The

Chicago Sun-Times discovered who he was, got him out of jail, and raised a fund for his rehabilitation. A job was secured for him in Los Angeles, where it was hoped that he might make a fresh start. Many organizations, including church groups, helped out.

Hayes thanked everybody gratefully, and said, "I know I'm cured of drinking now." But in less than a week he was arrested by Los Angeles police on the old charge. When he returned to Phoenix he received no hero's welcome. He told the reporter who met him: "I guess I'm just no good. I've had a lot of chances, but just when things started looking good I get that craving for whisky and foul up. I'm going back home for a while. Maybe after I'm around my family I'll be able to figure things out."

But the family home still did not have the answer. Across the road and across the fence which marks the Pima reservation, water runs in irrigation ditches. The desert is green with cotton, barley, wheat, alfalfa and citrus fruits, pasturage for sheep and cattle. But the water and the green fields are on the white man's side of the reservation fence.

He tried once, in 1950, to plead the case of his people before government officials in Washington. He asked "for freedom for the Pima Indians. They want to manage their own affairs, and cease being wards of federal government."

But what he was asking had become infinitely complicated. It involved acts of Congress, court decrees, a landowners' agreement, operation and maintenance requirements. So complicated had it become that the lawyers and the engineers and the administrators hired by the government had succeeded only in reducing by half the acreage which the Pima Indians, in their simple way, had cultivated, on which they had grown surpluses of grain to sell to hungry white men.

Ira Hayes, coming back home, looked at the mud-and-wattle house, the ramada standing to one side, a few poor outbuildings, and knew that he would not find the answer there. He found it on the cold ground in a cotton field.

VI

GOVERNMENT BY CONSENT

Just as settlement of the United States took place by compelling the Indians to accept European laws and practices pertaining to land, so also dominion over the tribes themselves was achieved by substituting the rule of the outsider for inherent self-rule.

And just as the Indians still retain bits and parcels of their original homeland, so also they still cling to shreds of the sovereignty which once was theirs.

Today, when Indians must look to the seat of government in Washington for the decisions which affect so many aspects of their lives, it is small wonder that they fall into the habit of thinking of themselves as powerless to act on their own.

The Navajo people have incorporated into their language the word "Washington," by which they convey all shades of meaning having to do with the white man's government; but even more eloquent frequently are the tones of the voice in which the word is uttered, signifying the speaker's contempt, bewilderment, or frustration. In this respect, the Navajo reflects the experiences of all Indians.

It is not surprising that Indians should have mingled feelings about the government of the United States. For there have been, in the history of government-Indian relations, two clear lines of thought, inconsistent with each other, mutually hostile, the net result of which through the years has been to nullify good intention.

In the one view, that of Chief Justice John Marshall: "America was inhabited by a distinct people, divided into separate nations, independent of each other, and of the rest of the world, and governing themselves by their own laws."[1] The opinion was written in 1832.

For the other view, we choose one expressed forty years later by the Commissioner of Indian Affairs, Francis A. Walker: "There is no question of national dignity, be it remembered, involved in the treatment of savages by a civilized power. With wild men, as with wild beasts, the question whether in a given situation one shall fight, coax, or run, is a question merely of what is easiest and safest." Walker elaborated on this point of view by commenting, "No one certainly will rejoice more heartily than the present Commissioner when the Indians of this country cease to be in a position to dictate, in any form or degree, to the government; when, in fact, the last hostile tribe becomes reduced to the condition of suppliants for charity."[2]

The question of which view was morally correct—the "separate nation" or the "wild beast" view—would be before the country for decision for many years.

The antecedents of the first view reach back to the beginnings of European discovery and settlement. Thus the officials of the Dutch West India Company in 1630 issued instruction as follows:

"The Patroons of New Netherland, shall be bound to purchase from the Lords Sachems in New Netherland, the soil where they propose to plant their Colonies, and shall acquire such right thereunto as they will agree for with the said Sachems."[3]

In similar vein Captain John Endecott, in charge of the first colonizing group sent out by the Massachusetts Bay Company, was instructed by the officers of that company: "Above all, we pray you to be careful that there be none in our precincts permitted to do any injury, in the least kind, to the heathen people; and if any offend in that way, let them receive due correction."

In part the attitude was born of expediency, as the letter to Captain Endecott further suggests: "If any of the savages pretend right of inheritance to all or any part of the lands granted in our patent, we pray you endeavor to purchase their title, that we may avoid the least scruple of intrusion."[4]

But expediency did not explain the whole motive of the

European going among the Indians. Thus, William Penn, in purchasing land from the Delaware Indians in 1682, explained through his negotiating agent: "I desire to enjoy it with your consent, that we may always live together as neighbors and friends."[5] Another Quaker, John Woolman, wrote in his *Journal* (1763): "A concern arose to spend some time with the Indians, that I might feel and understand their life and the spirit they live in, if happily I might receive some instruction from them, or they might in any degree be helped forward by my following the leading of truth among them."[6]

The experiences of the British government in attempting to develop equitable relations with the Indian tribes have an importance to us because they foreshadow the efforts made later by the United States government. The British effort consisted of attempts (1) to centralize authority in this field, (2) to improve the standards of conduct of traders doing business with Indian groups, and (3) to regularize the procedures of negotiating for land cessions.

The difficulties which confronted the British in these efforts are explained by a recent writer:

Colonial management of the savages had been inefficient because various colonial governors, traders and agents had often duplicated their labors and had never agreed upon a working system of cooperation or profit sharing. The seriousness of the Indian problem, after Braddock's defeat, demanded a straightforward, centralized policy. But, it may be pertinently asked, what experience had the European world in modern times in ruling so-called backward peoples? France had not governed the Indians although she had evolved a centralized trade organization. Frenchmen had lived among Indians and had traded with them, but they soon became more Indian than French. The Dutch had possessed themselves of a rich part of the far east, but the Dutch East India Company had remained exclusively a trading corporation. The failure of the Dutch to hold large possessions has been ascribed to this exclusively mercantile program.

The British, on the contrary, soon evolved a satisfactory imperialistic policy. Owing to the existence of the East India Company the assumption of responsibility by the government itself was gradual and progressive. It was really in America then that they were first confronted on a small scale with a task, which has never ceased to be present, of governing native peoples.[7]

In American history books the Albany Congress of 1754 is cited as one of the landmarks in the growth toward unity which ultimately led the colonies to stand together against the mother country. From the point of view of the British government, striving to centralize policy and authority in the field of Indian affairs, the Congress was a failure. The Board of Trade, which was responsible for colonial affairs, took the initiative in its own hands at that point and, among other actions, appointed a commander in chief (General Braddock) over all colonial and British forces in America, and two Indian agents to have over-all responsibility in the field of Indian affairs, one (Sir William Johnson) for the northern tribes, the other (Edmund Atkin) for the southern tribes. These two men were well informed, were respected by the Indians, and made great progress in reconciling points at issue which had developed between Indians and whites.

A recent study of the work carried on by Edmund Atkin gives insight into the problems faced by Atkin, and, for that matter, by Sir William Johnson in the north.

Atkin is quoted: "The importance of Indians is now generally known and understood. A doubt remains not, that the prosperity of our colonies on the continent, will stand or fall with our interest and favor among them. While they are our friends, they are the cheapest and strongest barrier for the protection of our settlements; when enemies, they are capable of ravaging in their method of war, in spite of all we can do, to render these possessions almost useless."

And at another place: "Some of the colonies have made no regulations at all in the Indian affairs; others have made different ones, and some but seldom if at all sent proper persons to look into them. But the management of them have often been left to traders, who have no skill in public affairs, are directed only by their own interests, and being generally the loosest kind of people, are despised and held in great contempt by the Indians as liars, and persons regarding nothing but their own gain."

He characterizes the Indians of his acquaintance in these words: "No people in the world understand and pursue their true national interests better than the Indians. How sanguinary so ever they are towards their enemies, from a misguided passion of heroism, and a love of their country; yet they are other ways truly humane, hospitable, and equitable. . . . In their public treaties, no people on earth are more open, explicit, and direct; nor are they excelled by any in the observance of them."[8]

The high-water mark of British achievement in this new and difficult field of human relations was the issuance of the Royal Proclamation of 1763—a document which reconciled the expedient needs of a government seeking to mitigate Indian hostilities (the Pontiac uprising was the immediate spark, although the Proclamation had been some time in the making) with an often expressed desire of the individual colonies and the mother country to deal honorably with the Indian people.

The terms of this Proclamation are of special interest because, in succeeding years, they had so direct an influence on actions taken by the United States government. First, it recognized that the Indian tribes were entitled to the peaceful possession of any lands which they had not formally sold or ceded; second, a boundary line was prescribed, following roughly the Appalachian watershed, beyond which settlement by white men was prohibited so long as the Indians held the lands; third, it required that persons who might have settled on Indian lands, through inadvertence or otherwise, remove immediately; and finally, it established a rule for the peaceful acquisition of future lands.[9]

The position of the United Colonies at the moment of breaking away from Britain was essentially identical with Britain's position in the previous decade. Britain had faced a formidable rival in France, each contending for control of North America, and each sensible of the fact that the Indians might be the deciding factor in determining which would prevail.

In 1775, the rebelling colonies faced England, and again each side knew that the Indians might be a decisive factor. American policy, then, as was England's earlier, was a compound of expedient need and a desire to put a good foot forward before the world.

So great was the need that, in the very weeks when George Washington was trying to organize an army to contain the British in Boston Harbor, the Continental Congress took steps to "secure and preserve" the friendship of the Indian nations.[10] It appointed a committee to negotiate with the Indians composed of Philip Schuyler, Patrick Henry, James Duane, James Wilson, and Philip Livingston. Following the recommendations of this committee, the Congress of July 12, 1775, resolved "That the securing and preserving the friendship of Indian nations, appears to be a subject of the utmost moment to these Colonies. . . ." Later in the summer the Congress dispatched an urgent message to the Six Nations (Iroquois), modeled after the best Indian oratory of the period: "Brothers, in our consultation we have judged it proper and necessary to send you this talk, as we are upon the same island, that you may be informed of the reasons of this great Council . . ." and concluding: "This is a family quarrel between us and old England . . . we desire you to remain at home, and not join on either side, but keep the hatchet buried deep."

It was a sore point that four out of the Six Nations took sides with the British (the Oneida and Tuscarora remained neutral), and there were some in Congress who insisted that Indian lands be confiscated in retaliation. Here expediency still prevailed. General Philip Schuyler and others persuaded Congress that to drive the Indians beyond the settled borders would be expensive, and was not necessary. The Indian Committee in October, 1783, recommended that negotiations be entered into with the Indians, in which the United States should seek "neither to yield nor to require too much," new territorial boundaries should be agreed upon, and general regulations should be established to regulate trade and control the movement of settlers.

General Schuyler's views found acceptance with General Washington. He agreed to a general boundary line between whites and Indians and opposed haphazard settlement of the new western country. The Indians would retire as game animals disappeared, and the lands they abandoned could be purchased at far less expense than the cost of war.

These views led to the adoption of an Ordinance for the Regulation of Indian Affairs (August 7, 1786), which created an Indian Department divided in two districts, northern and southern, and set up strict rules for the control of trade. A year later (July 13, 1787) the Ordinance for the Government of the Northwest Territory contained the declaration: "The utmost good faith shall always be observed towards the Indians, their lands and property shall never be taken from them without their consent; and in their property rights and liberty, they never shall be invaded or disturbed, unless in just and lawful wars authorized by congress; but laws founded in justice and humanity shall from time to time be made, for preventing wrongs being done to them, and for preserving peace and friendship with them."

Among the advisers to General Washington, who took account not only of expediency but of the judgment of men as well, was Henry Knox, who rose from the humdrum existence of a Boston bookseller to become one of Washington's ablest generals and, eventually, first Secretary of War.[11] Knox, too, gave thought to the advisability of raising an army to move against the Indians, this time in the Wabash River country. His letter to Washington of June 15, 1789, observed that two methods of dealing with the hostile Indians suggested themselves:

The first of which is by raising an army, and extirpating the refractory tribes entirely, or secondly by forming treaties of peace with them, in which their rights and limits be explicitly defined. . . .

In considering the first mode [a question arises] whether . . . the United States have a clear right, consistently with the principles of justice and the laws of nature, to proceed to destruction or expulsion of the savages, on the Wabash, supposing force for that object easily obtainable. It is presumable, that a nation solicitous of establishing its character on the broad basis of justice, would not only hesitate at, but reject every proposition to benefit itself, by the injury of any neighboring community, however contemptible and weak it might be, either with respect to its manners or power. The Indians being the prior occupants, possess the right of the soil. It cannot be taken from them unless by their free consent, or by the right of conquest in case of a just war.

Out of such beginnings, in part a maneuvering for survival and in part a moral concern, finally emerged the basic edifice of American policy toward the Indian people.

Chief Justice John Marshall was the principal architect of this policy, as he was the designer of so much of the constitutional law of this nation. He wrote three major decisions dealing directly with Indian questions: *Johnson's and Graham's Lessee* v. *McIntosh* (1823), *Cherokee Nation* v. *Georgia* (1831), and *Worcester* v. *Georgia* (1832).[12]

The first of these decisions, discussed in a previous chapter, dealt with the nature of Indian land title. It concluded that the Indians had a possessory right in the land, while the United States, as successor to Great Britain's claims as well as to the claims of other European nations, had the ultimate legal title.

The second decision examined the question whether an Indian tribe was in fact a foreign state competent to bring an action against one of the United States in a federal court. He decided in the negative, for these reasons:

Though the Indians are acknowledged to have an unquestionable, and heretofore unquestioned, right to the lands they occupy, until that right shall be extinguished by a voluntary cession to the government, yet it may well be doubted, whether those tribes which reside within the acknowledged boundaries of the United States can, with strict accuracy, be denominated foreign nations. They may, more correctly, perhaps, be denominated domestic dependent nations. . . . They are in a state of pupilage; their relations to the United States resembles that of a ward to his guardian. They look to our government for protection; they rely upon its kindness and its power; appeal to it for relief of their wants; and address the President as their Great Father.

In the last of these opinions the status of an Indian tribe in United States law was further examined, and it was held that "The Indian nations had always been considered as distinct, independent, political communities, retaining their original natural rights . . . the settled doctrine of the law of nations is, that a weaker power does not surrender its independence—its right to self-government—by associating with a stronger, and taking its protection. A weak state, in order to provide for its safety, may place itself under the protection of one more powerful, without stripping itself of its right of government, and ceasing to be a state."

These opinions have come down through the years without basic modification, although the principles involved have been applied in literally hundreds of later situations. Elaboration and specification have expanded the field, but the principles continue to govern.

Examples of how these opinions have been elaborated are briefly noted. In *United States* v. *Shoshone Tribe* (1938), the Court examined further the question of what is meant by possessory right or right of occupancy, as against the legal title held by the United States. The specific question was whether Indian title included timber and minerals, or was limited to such surface resources as the Indians commonly used. The Court was explicit in saying, "Although the United States retained the fee, and the tribe's right of occupancy was incapable of alienation or being held otherwise than in common, that right is as sacred and as securely safeguarded as is fee simple absolute title. . . . The Shoshone Tribe had the right that has always been understood to belong to Indians, undisturbed possessors of the soil from time immemorial."[13] That right included all elements of value above and below the surface.

In *United States as Guardian of Hualapai* v. *Santa Fe Pacific Railroad Company* (1941), another area of doubt was cleared away by the Supreme Court. In this case, Congress had granted lands to the Santa Fe Railroad for a right of way which ran through the Hualapai Indian Reservation in Arizona. At the time of the grant in 1866, the Hualapai Reservation did not exist, it having been created by Act of Congress in 1883. In 1925, the General Land Office of the Department of Interior started action to issue patents to the lands granted to the railroad company, but the Indians objected on the grounds that the land really belonged to them by right of aboriginal title. Two lower courts held against the Indians, and when the case reached the Supreme Court the attorney general of Arizona argued that "Any suggestions by this court that Indian tribes might have rights in property enforceable in a court of law by the mere fact of occupancy would at least cast a cloud upon the title to the major portion of Arizona."

The Court was not deterred by this argument, and required the trial court to make a finding of fact as to the extent of land actually occupied by the Indians prior to the time of the grant to the railroad company. As a result of the findings of the trial court, 509,000 acres were restored to the Hualapai Indians.[14]

Against this clear line of a developing policy, aimed at securing the Indian people in the possession of their lands and in their rights, as "domestic dependent nations," to govern their internal affairs, and through their institutions and social systems to adjust their lives to the changed conditions brought on by the nation that grew up around them, it is necessary to relate that contrary forces worked to nullify such development.

VII

MORALITY WITHIN LIMITS

THE public official who most consistently opposed the views developed by Chief Justice Marshall was Andrew Jackson. In time, Jackson's influence gained the ascendancy in both the executive and legislative branches of the government, and resulted in major retreats from the forthright declaration of policy contained in the Northwest Ordinance of 1787.

Jackson had time and sentiment on his side. As a statesman grown to influence in the country beyond the Appalachian watershed, he was concerned for the growth of the West. He spoke for thousands of land-hungry families, anxious to rid the forests and clearings of the title pretensions of the red man.

Just after President Monroe took office in March, 1817, Jackson began to press for acceptance of his point of view. The opinion that Indians were entitled to occupy the land until their right was purchased from them in lawful negotiations was not practical. Too many Indians were refusing to negotiate. The pinch came when, during and after the Revolutionary War, the seaboard colonies yielded their claims to the western lands, to which, by their vaguely written charters, they were presumably entitled. The lands yielded became part of the public domain of the new nation. Land speculators and earnest families in search of new homes made purchases in the relinquished areas, only to find that the Indian title had not been quieted and they were out of pocket. This was an intolerable application of moral principle.

So Jackson wrote to Monroe: "Within the chartered limits of the State of Tennessee a great portion [of land] was sold early in 1783 to redeem the public debt of the Revolution and patents have been issued for the same. The individuals purchasing expected immediate possession. They believed that the State of North Carolina possessed a good title as no other was set up or acknowledged; and by the Treaty of Peace Great Britain acknowledged [herself] conquered. . . . The policy of government in open violation of the Constitution, which secures property from being taken for public use without just compensation being made, has by law, prevented the individuals from taking possession of their lands, and reserved them for hunting grounds for the Indians. The game being destroyed as acknowledged by all, the right of possession, granted to the Indians for the purpose of hunting ceases, and justice, sound policy, and the constitutional rights of the citizen, would require its being resigned to him.

It may be asked how this land is to be obtained from the Indians, they having refused to relinquish their claim to the commissioners lately appointed and authorized to make this purchase from them, one of whom, I was. . . . I have long viewed treaties with the Indians an absurdity not to be reconciled to the principles of our government. The Indians are the subjects of the United States, inhabiting its territory and acknowledging its sovereignty, then is it not absurd for the sovereign to negotiate by treaty with the subject? I have always thought, that congress had as much right to regulate by acts of legislation, all Indian concerns, as they had of territories; there is only this difference, that the inhabitants of territories, are citizens of the United States and entitled to all the rights thereof; the Indians are subjects and entitled to their protection and fostering care, the proper guardian of this protection and fostering care is the legislature of the Union.

To this might be opposed the policy and practice of government so long pursued towards them, to which I would answer, that this policy grew out of the weakness of the arm of government . . . and not from rights acknowledged to be possessed by them."[1]

Monroe was aware of the moral issue involved but he was prepared to look for some compromise. Writing to Jackson a few months later, he indicated how this compromise might be rationalized: "The view which you have taken . . . is new but very deserving of attention. The hunter or savage state requires a greater extent of territory to sustain it, than is compatible with the progress and just claims of civilized life . . . and must yield to it. . . . Within our limits, where the Indian title is not extinguished, our title is good against European powers only, and it is by treaties with the former that our limits are formed. . . . A compulsory process seems to be necessary, to break their habits, and civilize them, and there is much cause to believe that it must be resorted to, to preserve them."[2]

The immediate result of Jackson's personal and official efforts was the Indian Removal Act of 1830, already discussed. The long-run result, forty years later, was the declaration by Congress of March 3, 1871, that "Hereafter no Indian nation or tribe within the territory of the United States shall be acknowledged or recognized as an independent nation, tribe, or power with whom the United States may contract by treaty."

This legislative fiat was reached without benefit of public debate. It was attached as a legislative rider to the appropriation act supplying funds for the Department of Interior, hence it did not follow the usual legislative course of a bill introduced and considered on its merit. It was a price exacted by the House of Representatives to provide funds requested by the Senate in carrying out the terms of certain treaties with Indian tribes.

The legislative branch of the government had reached the decision that the Indians were no longer competent to rule themselves, and must be ruled instead by a body of white men sitting in a great stone house a thousand miles from the nearest brush and bark wigwam. Few if any Indians were eligible to vote in the year 1871, and so were not able to share in the naming of any of the lawmakers who would pass laws affecting their property and their lives. But no one seemed to be concerned just then.

The concern, rather, was in substituting a "compulsory process" for the natural processes of human growth. Perhaps it could be reduced to a formula involving time sequences. An Indian tribe might be entitled to assert its rights for thirty days, but after that it had no rights.

Count Alexis de Tocqueville, observing a band of Choctaw Indians crossing the Mississippi River in the winter of 1831, remarked: "The Indians, in the little which they have done, have unquestionably displayed as much natural genius as peoples of Europe in their greatest undertakings; but nations as well as men require time to learn, whatever may be their intelligence and their zeal. . . . The Indians have been ruined by a competition which they had not the means of sustaining. They were isolated in their own country, and their race only constituted a little colony of troublesome strangers in the midst of numerous and dominant people."[3]

VIII

THE DEVELOPING DILEMMA[1]

The Bureau of Indian Affairs was required to develop and become a responsible public agency within the ambiguities of conflicting doctrines and political forces. The men who have headed the Bureau, as Commissioner, generally have reflected political temper rather than public principle, and it could hardly be otherwise since the Commissioner is the appointee of the administration in power.

Exceptional men have filled the position, it must be said; though it was the rare occasion that the exceptional man was searched out or, if discovered, would accept the honor. The job of Indian Commissioner has always been an onerous one; the remuneration has never been commensurate with the protean skills required of the incumbent; and the chances for ignominious failure have always been a deterrent to the conscientious office seeker.

Management of Indian affairs was at first a function of the War Department, created by act of Congress of August 7, 1789. The act authorized the Secretary of the Department to handle such Indian matters as might be "entrusted to him by the President of the United States." In those first years the routine of dealing with Indian tribes fell not upon the Secretary of War, but upon the managers of the government trading houses created in 1796 and continued until 1822. These agents likewise were appointed by the President and their task was to supply trade goods at a fair price, to offer a fair price for furs in exchange, and generally to act as representatives of the United States.

The government trading houses fell victim to the demands of

private enterprise; but even before they were discontinued, a program of Indian education was authorized, in 1819, when an annual appropriation of $10,000 was directed to be used for the "civilization of the Indians."

When a Bureau of Indian Affairs was created within the War Department in 1824 by the order of the then Secretary, Calhoun, the staff consisted of the Commissioner, Thomas L. McKenney, who had been the last superintendent of Indian trade, one chief clerk, and one assistant.

Statutory authority for the office of Commissioner of Indian Affairs was contained in the act of July 9, 1832, the appointment to be by the President, with the consent of the Senate. He was to have "direction and management of all Indian affairs, and of all matters arising out of Indian relations," under the direction of the Secretary of War and subject to regulations prescribed by the President.

Two years later, the act of June 30, 1834, established the Bureau of Indian Affairs in the War Department. There it continued until transferred to the Department of the Interior when the latter was created by the Act of March 3, 1849. The Secretary of the Interior was authorized to "exercise the supervisory and appellate powers now exercised by the Secretary of the War Department, in relation to all the acts of the Commissioner of Indian Affairs."

Army officers continued to serve as agents in charge of Indian reservations, and for at least twenty years after the creation of the Interior Department there was intermittent, and sometimes bitter, debate as to whether the management of Indian affairs belonged in a civilian or military branch of the government. Partly this was occasioned by the alarms and excursions of the Indian wars of that period, but in a deeper sense it reflected the unresolved question whether Indians were reasonable men capable of learning or wild beasts responsive only to a show of force.

The details of administration of the 170 years of relations between the United States and the Indian people make tedious reading today. But if we are to understand why the Indian people are apprehensive of proposals put forward in their behalf—why the word "Washington" inspires such varied emotional responses—then we are concerned at least to know what was attempted to better Indian conditions, the reasons behind the efforts, and the results. Given such knowledge, and given an inclination to learn from the past, it may be possible to improve future action.

The course of those years was not as true as a gun barrel, but it had a kind of inevitability. If the line of development were charted, it would not be a straight line between two points; it would be a meander, but still it arrived at a predictable point.

If the line is thought of as a chain of policy decisions, it begins in the act of Congress of August 7, 1789, reaffirming the "utmost good faith" guarantee of the Northwest Ordinance; and it concludes in House Concurrent Resolution 108 of the first session of the 83rd Congress (1953).

In the first years of that long interval, Congress, the policy maker, was concerned with holding the friendship of the Indian tribes. The European powers in those early years were still forces to be reckoned with on the continent and were suspected, indeed known, to be conspiring with the Indian tribes, seeking their trade and possibly their support in military action. The early legislation dealt almost exclusively with the regulation of trade, protecting the Indians against unscrupulous adventurers and mischief-makers. The United States was never interested in trade for profit, as was France, and to a lesser extent England; the lawmakers were not opposed to profit taking by private enterprises, but they wanted to avoid giving cause for complaint on account of unfair trading practices.

Another objective of the first legislation was the protection of the country from nationalists of other countries who might stir up trouble among the Indian tribes. Thus the Act of January 17, 1800, provided: "In case any citizen or other person shall alienate, or attempt to alienate the confidence of the Indians from the government of the United States, or from any such person or persons as are, or may be employed and entrusted by the President of the United States, as a commissioner . . . [or] agent . . . he shall forfeit a sum not exceeding $1,000, and be imprisoned not exceeding twelve months."

The first attempt to write a general statute governing Indian affairs resulted in the Trade and Intercourse Act of June 30, 1834—the date of the act providing for the organization of the Bureau of Indian Affairs. These two basic statutes followed recommendations submitted to Congress by Lewis Cass, the Secretary of War.

The recommendations supply insight into the times, as in the following passage:

> The Indians, for whose protection these laws are proposed, consist of numerous tribes, scattered over an immense extent of country, of different languages, and partaking of all the forms of society in the progression from the savage to an approximation to the civilized. With the emigrant tribes we have treaties, imposing duties of a mixed character, recognizing them in some sort as dependent tribes, and yet obligating ourselves to protect them, even against domestic strife, and necessarily retaining the power so to do. With other tribes we have general treaties of amity; and with a considerable number we have no treaties whatever. To most of the tribes with whom we have treaties, we have stipulated to pay annuities in various forms. These, though a part of the consideration of the cessions of land, are intended to promote their improvement and civilization, and which may now be considered as the leading principle of this branch of our legislation.

The 1834 act refrained from intruding upon areas of jurisdiction which belonged to tribal government. Thus, the act provided that United States criminal law would extend to the Indian country, but only with respect to acts committed by non-Indians against other non-Indians. The Secretary of War explained: "It will be seen that we cannot, consistently with the provisions of some of our treaties, and of the territorial act, extend our criminal laws to offences committed by or against Indians, of which the tribes have exclusive jurisdiction. . . . It is not perceived that we can with any justice or propriety extend our laws to offences committed by Indians against Indians, at any place within their own limits."

Again, in the matter of making annuity payments under treaty terms, the Secretary's report observed: "The payments are required, by the terms of the treaties, to be paid to the tribe as a political body capable of acting as a nation; and it would seem, as a necessary consequence, that the payments should be made to the constituted authorities of the tribe."

Still another section of the law contained a directive for administrative action which was rarely honored in succeeding years. It read: "Where any of the tribes are, in the opinion of the Secretary of War, competent to direct the employment of their blacksmiths, mechanics, teachers, farmers, or other persons engaged for them, the direction of such persons may be given to the proper authority of the tribe."

The commissioners of Indian Affairs in those early years made no notable contributions to the formulation of policy, to judge from their annual reports. The first of these, Thomas L. McKenney, urged the building of schools as the best means of "keeping the peace among the Indians themselves and attaching them to us." Other commissioners were of the same mind, though regular academic training from the first was viewed with skepticism. Thus, Commissioner Crawford (1838): "To teach a savage man to read, while he continues a savage in all else, is to throw seed on a rock. Manual labor schools are what the Indian condition calls for."

Most of the commissioners in this period were satisfied to support the national policy of transporting the tribes beyond the Mississippi River.

During these years also, one finds repeated references in the commissioners' reports to the idea of individualizing the tribal landholdings as a civilizing device. Commissioner Crawford was one of the first to remark that "common property and civilization cannot coexist."

In 1853, Commissioner Manypenny, reporting on negotiations he had conducted with various tribes, wrote: "With but few exceptions, the Indians were opposed to selling any part of their lands, as announced in their replies to speeches of the commissioners. Finally, however, many tribes expressed their willingness to sell, but on the condition that they could retain tribal reservations on their present tracts of land. . . . The idea of retaining reservations, which seemed to be generally entertained, is not deemed to be consistent with their true interests, and every good influence ought to be exercised to enlighten them on the subject. If they dispose of their lands, no reservation should, if it can be avoided, be granted or allowed."

Four years later, Commissioner Denver recommended: "Their reservations should be restricted so as to contain only sufficient land to afford them a comfortable support by actual cultivation, and should be properly divided and assigned to them, with the obligation to remain upon and cultivate the same."

These considerations were entering into policy by 1859, as reported by Secretary of the Interior Thompson: "At present, the policy of the government is to gather the Indians upon small tribal reservations, within the well defined exterior boundaries of which small tracts of land are assigned, in severalty, to the individual members of the tribe, with all the rights incident to an estate in fee simple, except the power of alienation. This system, wherever it has been tried, has worked well, and the reports of superintendents and agents give a most gratifying account of the great improvement which it has effected in the character and habits of those tribes which have been brought up under its operation."

By the 1860's, secretaries and commissioners alike were recommending the abandonment of treaty making. Thus, Secretary Caleb B. Smith in 1862 observed: "It may well be questioned whether the government has not adopted a mistaken policy in regarding the Indian tribes as quasi-independent nations, and making treaties with them for the purchase of the lands they claim to own. They have none of the elements of nationality; they are within the limits of the recognized authority of the United States and must be subject to its control. The rapid progress of civilization upon this continent will not permit the lands which are required for cultivation to be surrendered to savage tribes for hunting grounds. Indeed, whatever may be the theory, the government has always demanded the removal of the Indians when their lands were required for agricultural purposes by advancing settlements."

And Commissioner Parker, himself part Indian, in 1869 urged

the same point of view: "The Indian tribes of the United States are not sovereign nations, capable of making treaties, as none of them have an organized government of such inherent strength as would secure a faithful obedience of its people in the observance of compacts of this character. They are held to be the wards of government, and the only title the law concedes to them to the lands they occupy or claim is a mere possessory one."

As noted above, Congress on March 3, 1871, discontinued treaty making and a system of agreements was substituted, the agreements being incorporated in statutes jointly passed by House and Senate. Even this practice was viewed with misgivings by Commissioner Edward P. Smith (1873): "This double condition of sovereignty and wardship involves increasing difficulties and absurdities, as the traditional chieftain, losing his hold upon his tribe, ceases to be distinguished for anything except for the lion's share of goods and monies which the government endeavors to send, through him, to his nominal subjects, and as the necessity of the Indians, pressed on every side by civilization, require more help and greater discrimination in the matter of distributing the tribal funds. So far, and as rapidly as possible, all recognition of Indians in any other relation than strictly as subjects of the government should cease."

Finally, the sentiment in favor of individualizing tribal landholdings, in official government circles as well as in the public view, resulted in the adoption of the General Allotment Act of February 8, 1887. The purposes and terms of this legislation will be discussed later; it is only observed here that throughout the discussions preceding the adoption of the act, the strongest sustaining argument in its favor was the civilizing influence it would have upon the first Americans.

Other purposes and objectives came to light immediately after the act's passage. As Commissioner Morgan reported in 1890: "The settled policy of the government [is] to break up reservations, destroy tribal relations, settle Indians upon their own homesteads, incorporate them into the national life, and deal with them not as nations or tribes or bands, but as individual citizens."

He further reported that in that single year, 17,400,000 acres, about one-seventh of all Indian land, had been acquired by the government. He thought it necessary to explain this development:

This might seem like a somewhat rapid reduction of the landed estate of the Indians, but when it is considered that for the most part the land relinquished was not being used for any purpose whatever, that scarcely any of it was in cultivation, that the Indians did not need it and would not be likely to need it at any future time, and that they were, as is believed, reasonably well paid for it, the matter assumes quite a different aspect. The sooner the tribal relations are broken up and the reservation system done away with the better it will be for all concerned. If there were no other reason for this change, the fact that individual ownership of property is the universal custom among civilized people of this country would be a sufficient reason for urging the handful of Indians to adopt it.

Two developments in this long course of events are of such importance as to compel more detailed analysis. These are the survey and report of Lewis Meriam and associates of the Institute for Government Research in 1928, and the adoption of the Indian Reorganization Act of June 18, 1934. They will be discussed in subsequent chapters.

Looking back over this record of years, it is obvious that the Indian side of the relationship is not indicated. One sees the Indians only through the eyes of men dealing with problems they rarely understand and who find themselves frustrated by the application of remedies that never seem to solve anything. Seen in this light, the Indians are shadowy forms, "savages," "poor creatures," "wild men," "the vanishing race." These are symbols, not substance.

Some awareness of substance was expressed by Francis Leupp, Commissioner from 1904 to 1909, when he wrote: "The task we must set ourselves is to win over the Indian children by sympathetic interest and unobtrusive guidance. It is a great mistake to try, as many good persons of bad judgment have tried, to start the little ones in the path of civilization by snapping all the ties of affection between them and their parents, and teaching them to despise the aged and non-progressive members of their families."

In such a statement is the beginning of insight; and the question then was: Would that insight grow? Would it ever be incorporated into official policy?

Let us continue an examination of the record.

IX

THE BANKRUPTCY OF
GREAT EXPECTATIONS

THE General Allotment Act was the culmination of proposals that had been aired by public officials and private citizens almost from the beginning of European settlement. For a people who could not conceive of landholding based on any system other than private tenure, it was inevitable that the idea should be advanced for the Indians. Europe and the white man's civilization had grown to greatness on such a system; therefore it was the proper answer for all people who struggled along with a less perfect arrangement.

So long as Indian tribes could hold the policy makers of the national government at arm's length, as they managed to do through the treaty process, they could determine for themselves what internal controls they chose to exercise over land or any other sphere of interest. But with that barrier removed in 1871, their defences were breached. The record of the years shows that individual Indians came, of their own accord, to an acceptance of the idea of private property in land and other chattels. But the process of individual growth and change was not acceptable. The policy makers wanted revolutions, and they wanted them to happen at once.

The idea of individual land allotment finds one of its earliest expressions in an action of the Massachusetts General Court of 1633, declaring: "For the further encouragement of the hopeful work amongst them, for the civilizing and helping them forward to Christianity, if any of the Indians shall be brought to civility, and shall come among the English to inhabit, in any of their plantations, and shall live there civilly and orderly, then such Indians shall have allotments amongst the English, according to the custom of the English in like case."

The justification for the policy was already fully stated by the elder John Winthrop in this same period: "That which is common to all is proper to none. This savage people ruleth over many lands without title or property; for they enclose no ground, neither have they cattell to maintayne it, but remove their dwellings as they have occasion, or as they can prevail against their neighbors. And why may not Christians have liberties to go and dwell amongst them in their waste lands and woods, leaving them such places as they have manured for their corn, as lawfully as Abraham did among the Sodomites? For God hath given to the sons of man a two-fold right to the earth; there is a natural right and a civil right. The first right was natural when men held the earth in common, every man settling and feeding where he pleased; then, as men and cattle increased, they appropriated some parcels of ground by enclosing and peculiar manurance, and this in tyme got them a civil right."[1]

After the establishment of the national government, Indians were encouraged to settle and make improvements upon individual holdings. Thomas McKenney, the first Commissioner, in urging appropriations for the support of Indian schools, proposed that as educated Indian youths "are qualified to enter upon a course of civilized life, sections of land be given to them, and a suitable present to commence with, of agricultural or other implements suited to the occupations in which they may be disposed to engage."

The rush to the West, temporarily halted during the Civil War, gathered speed and volume. The Homestead Act of 1862 provided for the transfer of a quarter-section of unoccupied public domain on payment of a nominal fee after five years of residence. Discharged soldiers and families from older settled areas swarmed into the western prairies to get their share of the "free" land. Close behind them pressed a tide of immigrants, their eyes lighted by new promises. By 1860, there were 4,136,000 foreign-born residents in a total national population of 31,443,000. A large percentage of these foreign-born had arrived during the 1840's and 1850's.

The discovery of gold, first on the Pacific coast, then in the Rocky Mountains, was an even sharper spur to hunger and ambition. In this same epoch, plans for the construction of trans-continental railroads were pushed in and out of Congress.

All of these pressures, in their separate and combined effects, resulted in demands to reduce Indian landholdings, to move Indian reservations out of the path of westward settlement. The General Allotment Act became the rationalization for all of these motives.[2]

By 1877, Carl Schurz, then Secretary of the Interior, recommended to Congress that allotments of land be made to heads of families on every reservation. His argument: "The enjoyment and pride of the individual ownership of property is one of the most effective civilizing agencies." A year later, Commissioner of Indian Affairs Hayt reported that the principle of allotment was "endorsed by all true friends of the Indian, as is evidenced by the numerous petitions to this effect presented to Congress from citizens of the various states."

The agent for the Yankton Sioux, in his annual report to the Commissioner for 1877, expressed the opinion that "As long as Indians live in villages they will retain many of their old and injurious habits. Frequent feasts, heathen ceremonies and dances, constant visiting—these will continue as long as people live together in close neighborhoods and villages. I trust that before another year is ended they will generally be located upon individual land or farms. From that date will begin their real and permanent progress."

In spite of the urgings of many groups and strong endorsements in official quarters, the adoption of the Allotment Act was not readily accomplished. First introduced formally in the closing session of the 45th Congress (1879), and reintroduced at the opening of the 46th Congress (1880), it encountered unexpectedly stiff opposition. Senator Teller of Colorado characterized the Senate version of the bill (introduced by Richard Coke of Texas) as "a bill to despoil the Indians of their lands and to make them vagabonds on the face of the earth." At another point in the debate, Teller admonished his colleagues: "If I stand alone in the Senate, I want to put upon the record my prophecy in this matter, that when thirty or forty years will have passed and these Indians shall have parted with their title, they will curse the hand that was raised professedly in their defence to secure this kind of legislation and if the people who are clamoring for it understood Indian character, and Indian laws, and Indian morals, and Indian religion, they would not be here clamoring for this at all."[3]

On the House side, where the Committee on Indian Affairs was considering similar legislation, a minority of the committee reported:

However much we may differ with the humanitarians who are riding this hobby, we are certain that they will agree with us in the proposition that it does not make a farmer out of an Indian to give him a quarter section of land. There are hundreds of thousands of white men, rich with the experiences of centuries of Anglo-Saxon civilization, who cannot be transformed into cultivators of the land by any such gift. . . . The real aim of this bill is to get at the Indian lands and open them up to settlement. The provisions for the apparent benefit of the Indian are but the pretext to get at his lands and occupy them. . . . If this were done in the name of greed, it would be bad enough; but to do it in the name of humanity, and under the cloak of an ardent desire to promote the Indian's welfare by making him like ourselves, whether he will or not, is infinitely worse.[4]

The proponents persisted. In 1885, and again in 1886, the policy was recommended by President Cleveland in his annual messages. General Sheridan gave his endorsement, as did the General Assembly of the Presbyterian Church in the U.S.A.

The Act was passed in the 49th Congress on February 8, 1887.

Senator Henry L. Dawes of Massachusetts, who, as chairman of the Senate Committee on Indian Affairs, managed the bill through its final skirmishes, was a man of unquestioned integrity. In his work as chairman, Edward Everett Hale said, "While he held the reins, nobody talked of dishonor in our dealings with the Indians."

He believed firmly in the aims and purposes of the legislation, both from a humanitarian point of view and as an economy measure in government. He reasoned:

> It seems to me that this is a self-acting machine that we have set going. If we only run it on the track it will work itself all out, and all these difficulties that have troubled my friend [Senator Teller] will pass away like snow in the springtime, and we will never know when they go. We will only know they are gone. . . . Suppose these Indians become citizens of the United States with this 160 acres of land to their sole use. What becomes of the Indian reservation? What becomes of the Indian Bureau? What becomes of all this machinery? They have all vanished, and the work for which they are created is all gone while you are making them citizens.[5]

The principal provisions of the Allotment Act were (1) The President of the United States was authorized to allot tribal lands in designated quantities—160 acres to each family head, eighty acres to each single person over eighteen years and each orphan under eighteen, and forty acres to each other single person under eighteen. (2) Each Indian would make his own selection; but if he failed or refused, a government agent would make the selection for him. (3) Titles were continued in trust for twenty-five years, or longer, at the President's discretion. (4) Citizenship was conferred upon all allottees and upon other Indians who abandoned their tribes and adopted "the habits of civilized life." (5) Surplus tribal lands remaining after allotment might be sold to the United States.

Those were the main working provisions, though other features were included.

The effects of the law were spectacular. In 1887, approximately 140,000,000 acres of land remained in Indian ownership. The legislation, together with amendments adopted in succeeding years, set up procedures which resulted in the loss of some 90,-000,000 acres in the next forty-five years.[6]

The principal mechanism for reducing Indian ownership was the provision permitting the government to purchase so-called surplus lands. Sales could also be made by allottees after the trust period had ended, and could be ordered by the government in heirship cases—the Secretary was given authority by subsequent legislation to probate Indian estates and compel settlement.

As it happened, the lands that went first were the most valuable: agricultural lands in the river valleys, rich grasslands on the high plains, virgin forests in the Great Lakes region. What remained was desert or semidesert.

A corollary effect, which perhaps had not been anticipated by the supporters of the legislation, was the division of allotments through heirship procedures. So long as the land remained in trust status, it could not be sold but must be held for the legal heirs. Although the Secretary had authority to sell estate lands, it very soon became physically impossible to keep abreast of the probate work involved. After an original allotment of 160 or 80 acres had passed through two or three generations of inheritors, the parcels became so small as to be economically useless.

Usually the reservation superintendent leased the entire plot of land and divided the rent proceeds among the heirs. The ridiculous situation developed in which a rental share amounted to less than the postage required to send the payment through the mails. A Pima Indian whose allotment amounted to twenty acres on the Gila River Reservation of Arizona died in 1926. His estate was shared by seventy-three persons. The largest interest amounted to one acre, while several persons received pieces of ground eleven feet square.

The Pine Ridge Sioux Reservation in South Dakota, established by treaty in 1868, contained 2,721,597 acres. Beginning in 1904, the land was divided into 8,275 individual allotments, accounting for 2,380,195 acres. Only 182,653 acres were classified as surplus and sold to the government, and 146,633 acres were allowed to remain in tribal ownership, most of it wasteland which no member would select and the government would not purchase.

By 1930, 655,000 acres had been fee-patented and sold by individuals. In that same year, 904,000 acres had passed into heirship status and most of that acreage, for reasons mentioned above, was leased out to non-Indians.

When the Sioux came to the reservation following their final defeat in 1876, they camped in great circles and later in smaller bands and family camps. The camps spread themselves along the creeks and sheltered areas, close to water and grass.

The government issued live cattle and the Sioux began a new existence as livestock operators. By 1885, there were 10,000 head of cattle on the open range; and by 1912, 40,000 head. The allotting of land started in 1904, dividing the open range into 160-acre tracts, and by 1916 the process was completed. Individuals were encouraged to fence their allotments, and the open range began to disappear.

The Indian agent who came to the reservation in 1900 remained for seventeen years and encouraged the cattle program. In the short space of a lifetime the Sioux, notorious in frontier history as buffalo hunters and warriors, achieved a remarkable transition. They prospered as cattlemen under the instruction of an interested superintendent and the employees he brought in.

Then came World War I and the demand for wheat to feed Europe. A new superintendent took charge in 1917 and he encouraged the Pine Ridge Indians to sell their cattle and lease the range to white men who would plant the land to wheat. The Indians had neither the inclination nor the experience for the new venture, but cattle prices were high and the inducement to sell was strong. In a single year of the new policy, the cattle were gone and almost the entire arable area of the reservation was under lease to white men.

A student of the Pine Ridge Sioux makes this appraisal: "The Indian's loss of the cattle herds was the greatest disaster that had befallen the Pine Ridge Indians since the vanishing of the buffalo. For the second time the basis of their economy and the foundation upon which their society rests, were swept from beneath them."[7]

The sale of the cattle and the lease money from the land produced an illusion of wealth and well-being. The Indians indulged in an orgy of spending. They traded herds of horses for automobiles. When the automobiles wore out, they had no means of transportation. The postwar depression brought an end to high wheat and high cattle prices, and the white men abandoned their leases. The Indians became dependent upon federal charity, as their fathers had been dependent when the buffalo vanished.

A second object lesson was provided by the Sisseton Sioux, also of South Dakota. At one time this branch of the great Dakota nation had occupied the fabulously rich agricultural lands in the Red River Valley in Minnesota. In 1872, they had been persuaded to sell 11,000,000 acres of this land at 10 cents an acre, and they were induced to move to their present location in northeastern South Dakota.

When the allotment law was adopted, the Sisseton Sioux still owned 918,000 acres. Of this total, 300,000 acres were allotted to 2,000 Indians and the "surplus" of 600,000 acres was sold to the United States.

By 1909, two-thirds of the land which had been allotted was owned by white men—the trusteeship had been removed and the land sold. Only 35,000 acres remained in the hands of the original allottees. More than 80,000 acres had been divided through heirship procedures into smaller and smaller plots.

But the Indians did not disappear with the land. The original 2,000 who received allotments in the 1890's had increased to 3,000 by 1946. Of this total number, only 500 had left the reservation and 2,500 were trying to live on the income derived by a few from their shrinking reserve.

An investigating subcommittee of the House Committee on Indian Affairs, during a tour covering many Indian reservations, stopped at Sisseton in 1944. The report of this subcommittee described the reservation as "One of the most disgraceful situations in America . . . a nasty bad housing situation, living under impossible conditions, worse than the places in which we keep livestock."

A member of the tribe spoke ruefully of conditions: "Our young people get married and have no place to go or no place to build a home, and so, supposing a certain relative was making his way pretty well, instead of the children going away and making their way, they go and double themselves up until the old man is finally broke."[8]

If the great expectation of the Allotment Act had been the complete separation of Indians from the land, then it came close to achieving that total purpose. However, that had never been the total purpose. Throughout all the discussions stress had been placed on the educational value of individualized ownership and the corollary value that would result from breaking up the solidarity of tribal existence.

Any appraisement of the act therefore must be on the basis of what it proposed to accomplish; in that light, the act failed completely. The Indians did not become farmers; neither did they assume the habits of white people. Tribal existence became more difficult, as at Sisseton, but it persisted. Old customs, old attitudes, old values persisted.

Even the economy in government operations did not materialize. This feature of the act was brought into sharp relief by Commissioner John Collier in testifying before Congress in 1934. He stated:

The Indians are continuing to lose ground, yet government costs must increase, while the Indians must still continue to lose ground unless the existing law be changed. Two-thirds of the Indians in two-thirds of the Indian country for many years have been drifting toward complete impoverishment. While being stripped of their property these same Indians cumulatively have been disorganized as groups and pushed to a lower social level as individuals. During this time when Indian wealth had been shrinking and Indian life had been diminishing, the cost of Indian administration in the identical areas has been increasing. Ruin for the Indian and still larger costs to the government are being insured by the existing system.[9]

It was not the statesmen in Congress or the private citizens outside of Congress who saw the true situation during the debates that led to the adoption of the General Allotment Act. Instead, it was a group of Indians meeting in 1887 in a so-called international council of Indian territory. Some nineteen tribes were represented by a total of fifty-seven representatives, who voted unanimously against allotment, and against the granting of railroad rights of way through their land.

The council said:

Like other people the Indian needs at least a germ of political idenity, some governmental organization of his own, however crude, to which his pride in manhood may cling and claim allegiance, in order to make true progress in the affairs of life. This peculiarity in the Indian character is elsewhere called "patriotism," the wise and patient fashioning and guidance of which alone will successfully solve the question of civilization. Exclude him from this and he has little else to live for. The law to which objection is urged does this by enabling any member of a tribe to become a member of some other body politic by electing and taking to himself the quantity of land which at the present time is the common property of all.[10]

X

MEASURING RESULTS

By the 1920's the evidence that Indian affairs had been badly managed became notorious. A full decade before a depression struck the nation, the Indian people were suffering the pangs of hunger. As rural people, they shared in the general dislocation of depressed farm prices and vanishing opportunity. But theirs were special problems, brought on by decisions in which their voices had been ignored.

A generation of children had grown to maturity since the first allotments were made, and there was no land for them. Administrative officials, many as purblind as Commissioner Morgan, could not foresee that the Indians would need land in addition to the acreages allotted to individuals.

However, the parent generation which received land was scarcely any better off than the landless children. The elders had no capital funds to invest in equipment or livestock and, their allotments being held in trust, they could not obtain commercial credit for operating the land. Their greatest lack was in training and experience. The government schools operated for their benefit still followed the patterns established in the early years of the Bureau, with emphasis on manual labor. This meant employment on school maintenance and housekeeping tasks, at the expense of both academic and formalized vocational training. Indian students completing the school courses were not trained for either farm or industrial occupations. In the matter of schools, as in the matter of the disposition of land, the Indians had not been partners in decision making.

The land situation came first to public attention. The Secretary of Interior, by a 1906 statute, had been authorized to remove trusteeship and issue a patent-in-fee "whenever he shall be satisfied that any Indian allottee is competent and capable of managing his or her affairs."

This authority was used sparingly until 1917, when Commissioner Cato Sells instituted a policy of "greater liberalism" in releasing Indians from trusteeship. As he phrased his policy, "Every Indian, as soon as he has been determined to be as competent to transact his own business as the average white man, shall be given full control of his property and have all his lands and monies turned over to him, after which he will no longer be a ward of the government."

In justification of his decision, he declared: "This is a new and far reaching declaration of policy. It means the dawn of a new era in Indian administration. It means that the competent Indian will no longer be treated as half ward and half citizen. It means reduced appropriations by the government and more self respect and independence for the Indian. It means the ultimate absorption of the Indian race into the body politic of the nation. It means, in short, the beginning of the end of the Indian problem."

Special competency commissions were created to carry out the changed policy, the duty of the commissions being to determine which Indians were competent to handle their affairs. During the four-year period, 1917–21, some 20,000 fee patents were issued to individual Indians, or more than double the 9,894 patents issued prior to 1917 under the authority of the legislation of 1906.

The Board of Indian Commissioners made an investigation of the matter in 1921.[1] This Board, created by act of Congress in 1869, was an independent body appointed by the President and consisted of ten men "eminent for intelligence and philanthropy, to serve without pecuniary compensation." The Board had no authority in the field of policy, but through the years it exerted great influence on the policy makers. It had, for example, strongly supported the Allotment Act. Now it was uneasy.

In explaining the reason for its study, the Board reported:

We have observed in our field work the widely dissimilar consequences of transforming dependent government Indian wards into independent citizens with unrestricted possession of their property. Some of the new citizens developed into self-supporting, prosperous members of their community; others quickly lost their lands and monies and degenerated into indolent parasites, living on the bounty of their relatives.

Because of such wide differences in resultant living conditions, there are in Congress, in the Department, and among citizens' divergent opinions as to the kind of policy that ought to be followed in releasing Indians from government supervision, opinions so widely apart as to be contradictory. The advocates of the several policies may be grouped as follows: those that insist that all Indians shall be "turned loose" immediately and those who believe that no more Indians, of this generation, at least, shall be entirely released from government supervision.

In conducting its study, the Board sent questionnaires to eighty-seven field employees, superintendents, field clerks, and extension agents, all of whom were in daily contact with the Indian people. These employees were stationed on reservations in Oklahoma, South Dakota, North Dakota, Wisconsin, Kansas, Montana, Idaho, Wyoming, and Washington, states in which 155,000 out of the 175,000 Indians who had received land allotments were located.

Of the eighty-seven employees interrogated, seventy-one, or better than 81 per cent, reported that the Indians who had received fee patents in a majority of cases (and some reported in all cases) had disposed of their lands and monies. The report stated: "The fee patent Indians either sold their property themselves or lost it through foreclosure because they failed to pay the interest or principal of the mortgage. Instead of becoming self supporting farmers on their own land they soon were landless and penniless citizens. In short, in a good majority of the cases, the issuance of patents-in-fee seems to be a short cut to the separation of freed Indians from their land and cash."

Only ten of the informants indicated that the Indians of their acquaintance had obtained some degree of success. But only four out of the ten were able to report that the Indians were in actual possession of their lands.

This information, and other evidence coming to the attention of the government, resulted in an abandonment of the "liberal" policy in 1921.

Another issue that brought Indian affairs into public attention in the 1920's was an attempt to divest the Pueblo Indians of New Mexico of extensive landholdings. For many years white men had trespassed on lands belonging to the Pueblo Indians; they had built houses and appropriated rangeland and water. In some cases, possibly, they had moved upon land which they considered public domain, being unaware of the Indian ownership. Upon seeking to perfect title, and learning that they were in fact on Indian land, they sought legislative relief, claiming good faith and the failure of the government to mark the boundaries of the Indian lands.

A willing ally was found in Senator Bursum of New Mexico, who in 1922 introduced a bill which would have legislated rights into existence for these white squatters and would have thrown upon the Indians the burden of proving that the lands were theirs. The Indians, at best, would have had a slight chance of proving legal title through the confusions of American, Mexican, and Spanish occupations leading back to their own prehistory.

In November 1922, all the Pueblos came together at Santo Domingo, the first time they had banded together since 1680, when they drove the Spanish out of New Mexico. The All-Pueblo Council issued an appeal to the American people, and in successive legislative duels succeeded, with public opinion on their side, in defeating the Bursum bill. Later they secured the creation of the Pueblo Lands Board, which established an equitable procedure for determining land ownership in areas of dispute.[2]

The climate of public opinion created by such incidents led the Secretary of the Interior, Hubert Work, in 1926 to request the Institute for Government Research (Brookings Institution) to undertake a thorough economic and social study of Indian conditions. Lewis Meriam gathered a staff of advisers from the fields of law, economics, health, sociology, education, and agriculture and this group studied not only field conditions, but reviewed files and records and much of the history of Indian affairs. The result was a report of findings which provided, for the first time, a sober and searching analysis of what had happened to the Indian people under the government's trusteeship and proposed a number of basic recommendations.[3] In its general terms, the survey found that:

Most of the Indians were poor, many extremely poor.

The general health of the Indians was bad and their living, housing, and sanitary conditions were conducive to the development and spread of disease.

Tuberculosis and trachoma were prevalent to a distressing degree; the death rate and infant mortality rate were high.

In an economic sense, the Indians were backward; insufficient incomes, low standards of living, and an apathetic attitude toward progress were general.

The Indians were not yet adjusted to the new economic and social conditions confronting them.

They had little knowledge of the value of money and land.

The intermittent and generally small incomes from land sales, leases, and per capita payments from tribal funds encouraged idleness and retarded progress.

And it found too much evidence of suffering and discontent to subscribe to the belief that the Indians were satisfied with their conditions.

Looking for the causes back of these conditions, it found many contributing factors, and in the forefront was the allotment policy:

Not accompanied by adequate instruction in the use of property, it has largely failed in the accomplishment of what was expected of it. It has resulted in much loss of land and an enormous increase in the details of administration without a compensating advance in the economic ability of the Indians. . . . It almost seemed as if the government assumed that some magic in individual ownership of property would in itself prove an educational civilizing factor, but unfortunately this policy had for the most part operated in the opposite direction. Individual ownership in many instances permitted Indians to sell their allotment and to live for a time on the unearned income resulting from the sale.

Of the general economic situation of the Indian people the survey team found that "Even under the best conditions it is doubtful whether a well rounded program of economic advancement framed with due consideration of the natural resources of the reservation has anywhere been thoroughly tried out. The Indians often say that programs change with superintendents. Under the poorest administration, there is little evidence of anything which could be termed an economic program."

And in a further finding: "The Indian Service has not appreciated the fundamental importance of family life and community activities in the social and economic development of a people. The tendency has been rather toward weakening Indian family life and community activities than toward strengthening them."

Of the service programs available to the Indian people, the report found, in the field of health: "For some years it has been customary to speak of the Indian medical service as being organized for public health work, yet fundamentals of sound public health work are still lacking. . . . Special hospital equipment, such as x-ray, clinical laboratory, and special treatment facilities is generally lacking. . . . No sanatorium in the Indian service meets the minimum requirements of the American Sanatorium Association."

And in the field of education, the survey reported: "The work of the government directed toward the education and advancement of the Indian himself, as distinguished from the control and conservation of his property, is largely ineffective. . . . The survey staff finds itself obliged to say frankly and unequivocally that the provisions for the care of Indian children in boarding schools are grossly inadequate."

The recommendations for policy and action submitted by the survey team were as carefully stated as were their findings of fact. Generally, the recommendations followed no theoretical framework but were based on realistic appraisals of the legal and social responsibilities of the United States and the abilities and aspirations of the Indian people.

The underlying assumption on which all recommendations were based was a sound one. It stated: "The fundamental requirement is that the task of the Indian Service be recognized as primarily educational in the broadest sense of the word, and that it be made an efficient educational agency, devoting its main energies to social and economic advancement of the Indians, so that they may be absorbed into the prevailing civilization or be fitted to live in the presence of that civilization at least in accordance with a minimum standard of health and decency."

To bring about this fundamental objective, the report offered a number of recommendations, of which the following are particularly notable.

Recognizing the complex economic, social, and legal nature of the Indian situation, the report cited, as a "first outstanding need of the Indian Service," the creation of a planning and development division. As visualized by the survey staff, this division would advise the Commissioner of Indian Affairs in matters requiring technical or scientific knowledge of particular problems; subject to approval by the Commissioner, it would formulate programs and develop policies as guides to administrative operations and would co-operate with state and local authorities in planning joint undertakings; personnel of such a division would visit schools and agencies to offer technical assistance and advice to field employees and report to the Commissioner on the effectiveness of field operations; and further, the division would assist the Commissioner in holding hearings and investigating matters of special complaint involving problems of a technical nature.

The division would consist of professionally trained and experienced people in the fields of health, education, agriculture, animal husbandry, production and marketing of native Indian products, vocational guidance and placement, family and community life, social services, and law. In addition, the division would utilize consultants drawn from federal and state agencies, colleges and universities, private organizations, and individuals in the fields of social science and industry.

Recommendations for improving the organization and operations of the Indian Field Service were stressed as a second priority. The report referred to three general conditions prevailing in the Indian Service which discouraged effort and defeated programs:

The overwhelming administrative difficulty has arisen from the effort to operate the service upon an exceptionally low salary scale. In order to fill positions, when the salary scale is low, resort is almost invariably taken to the device of low entrance qualifications.

Every effort should be exerted to hold transfers of superintendents to a minimum and to provide for rewarding successful work on a small reservation by higher salary on that reservation. Too much emphasis can hardly be laid on the necessity for a superintendent to know his Indians and have their confidence, and that is something which cannot be done in a day.

Persons of high qualifications cannot be expected to enter and remain in the Indian Service unless material improvement is made in living and working conditions. The government must appreciate that at best conditions will be hard, especially for employees with families. The living quarters furnished should invariably be reasonably comfortable.

The survey revealed also that the service was weak "in personnel trained and experienced in educational work with families and communities," and that everywhere there was a "lack of trained subordinate personnel in immediate contact with the Indians."

The report offered recommendations to meet these conditions. It proposed "a fairly wide salary range for each superintendency, with a minimum in the neighborhood of the present salaries and with a maximum materially higher, as much as a third to a half higher would not be in the least unreasonable. Efficient and able superintendents with fine records and long service should be advanced to the maximum. The range between the minimum salary and the maximum salary should be especially wide in the case of the smaller jurisdictions."

At another place, the recommendation was: "In establishing the qualifications for entrance into the service two highly important factors will have to be taken into consideration despite the probable impossibility of establishing any formal civil service tests for them. They are, (1) character and personality, and (2) ability to understand Indians and get along with them."

With a more efficient field staff and operating conditions it would be possible, in the view of the survey staff, to achieve "maximum practical decentralization of authority so that to the fullest extent initiative and responsibility may be vested in the local officers in direct contact with the Indians."

Much more is contained in the Meriam survey. In some fields it was quite detailed in its findings and recommendations; but enough has been indicated of the fundamental purposes supported by the report. It was not a complete blueprint for action, but it was the first attempt to view the whole field of Indian needs by a body of disinterested and competent private citizens.

Scientists had been studying Indians for some years, but generally their studies resulted in contributions to ethnography and probably would not have been of much practical help to an Indian Service field employee, even if he knew about and attempted to read the material. The survey staff might not know about kinship systems or the occurrence of the glottal stop in certain Indian languages, but they knew about the place of the family in most societies and the influence of the community in the development of the individual; they could detect where Indian Service policy was defeating its purposes by destroying the very institutions which could make for the successful adjustment of the Indian people.

The survey represented an attempt to bring intelligence and objectivity into the administration of Indian affairs. What happened?

Certain immediate effects were noteworthy. In the administration which began in 1929, two prominent members of the Quaker faith, Charles J. Rhodes and J. Henry Scattergood, were appointed Commissioner and Assistant Commissioner, respectively. In education and health services, especially, their administration made significant changes of policy and practice, in directions indicated by the Meriam recommendations.

They obtained from Congress increased appropriations for education of from $3,000,000 in 1929 to more than $12,000,000 in 1932.

The concept of the function of education was equally significant, as reported by the Commissioner in 1931:

The purpose of education for any indigenous peoples of the present day is to help these peoples, both as groups and as individuals, to adjust themselves to modern life, protecting and preserving as much of their own way of living as possible, and capitalizing their economic and cultural resources for their own benefit and their contribution to modern civilization. Accordingly, if the Indian Service were starting afresh on a task of Indian education, with what is now known of the processes of change and adjustments through schools and other agencies, it would undoubtedly begin with the Indian people in their own environment or in some comparable environment in which they could develop their own resources. . . . But we are not starting afresh, and cannot; one kind of a philosophy and one kind of a system have been established a long time. The basic Indian Service educational problem, therefore, is to work over from a more or less conventional institutional conception of education to one that is local and individual. It means abandoning boarding schools wherever possible, eliminating small children from the larger boarding schools, setting up day schools or making arrangements with local public schools to receive these children, providing the necessary family follow-up for such children, and directing the boarding schools into specialized purposes, at least partly vocational.[4]

In a footnote to the section on education, Commissioner Rhodes considerably enlarged the view of his immediate task:

The Indian education problem in the United States is not an isolated problem, but one of a series of situations involving indigenous peoples throughout the world. The United States has more of these situations than it has cared to recognize in any effective way—Alaska has Indians and Eskimos, and in Puerto Rico, the Hawaiian Islands, the Philippines, Guam, Samoa, and the Virgin Islands, the same problem of a native, or at least a different racial group, presents itself, to say nothing of the millions of Negroes in continental United States. That the same situation is recognized elsewhere in the world is suggested by the programs in South Africa, Mexico, and Peru. . . . The determination of a program of Indian education in continental United States and Alaska, therefore, involves more than a few hundred thousand American Indians—it would have significance for the United States and possibly to some extent for the rest of the world.

At least some aspects of the recommendation to create a planning and development division were met by an administrative reorganization which became effective March 30, 1931. The Commissioner reported that "Directors of high professional and technical ability have been placed in charge of the five field divisions of health, education, agricultural extension and industry, forestry, and irrigation. These are grouped under two assistants to the commissioners: one in charge of human relations, and the other in charge of property. . . ."

Of the basic need for a land reform, however, little was accomplished during the 1929–33 administration. Basic legislation had first to be obtained, and Commissioner Rhodes had no success in securing help in Congress. In fact, by the end of his administration, he was severely under attack by such men as Senator King of Utah for the increased appropriations for Indian affairs which had been enticed out of Congress in a period of growing national depression. The land reforms would have to come later.

XI

The Indians Effort to

REDEEMING THE PAST

John Marshall wrote in *Cherokee Nation* v. *Georgia* that the relation of the Indian tribes to the United States "resembles that of a ward to his guardian." From this analogy grew a fearful regimentation of the Indian people: acts of Congress, aimed at correcting specific abuses, outlived the day of their need and remained to limit or to compel action; regulations of the Secretary of the Interior, with the passing of years, came to have the primacy of statutory law and to have its same compulsive effects. The initial intent was not to subject the Indian people to the proliferating controls which ultimately consumed them. Certainly Marshall did not contemplate such a result when he used his analogy. His word "resembles" is indicative of the limited sense in which he introduced the wardship idea. Like a ward, the tribes looked to the United States "for protection," relied upon the government's "kindness and power." He did not mean that the Indians had turned over their persons and their estates for management, as if they were legal wards in fact.

The framers of the United States Constitution, in authorizing Congress to regulate commerce with the Indian tribes and empowering the President and Senate to engage in treaty making, did not contemplate the result. The character of official actions and the nature of the discussions which took place between the individuals involved in the writing of the Constitution make clear that the intention was coexistence with the Indian people.

The legislation enacted in the first decades usually was limited to the fulfillment of tribal treaties. The authority for such legislation was the constitutional authority of the Congress to carry out treaty obligations. The Indian Removal Act of 1830 was an exception to the general practice, but even in this declaration of policy the language was permissive, not compulsory. The President was authorized to enter into treaties by which the eastern tribes would agree to move west of the Mississippi River. Force was ultimately used, but that was a decision of the executive branch exceeding the scope of the legislation. Characteristically, also, the early legislation was addressed to Indian tribes, not to the individual Indian.

The refusal by Congress in 1871 any longer to recognize Indian tribes for treaty purposes brought to a close that first epoch of government-Indian relations. The War of 1812 had long ago ended the threat of alliances between European powers and Indian tribes; and thereafter, as Jackson had protested for his frontier society, treaties became an "absurdity."

In the 1860's the volume of Indian legislation increased, and some of it intruded the power of the United States in internal tribal affairs. An act of 1862 provided that a chief or headman might be removed from office as a punitive measure. Legislation of this nature increased sharply after 1871, and the effects of legislation in time penetrated every sphere of tribal, family, and individual interests. Regulations written to effect the purposes of legislation multiplied the opportunities for directing and controlling Indian action.

One of the first actions of the New Deal Congress was to repeal, in 1934, twelve statutes, several of which were more than a hundred years old.[1] Among these were prohibitions against sending or carrying seditious messages to Indians or inciting Indians to revolt, which in later years had been used on occasion to suppress opposition to government policies; another law empowered superintendents to remove persons not legally on the reservation, to employ the military if necessary, and to impose a fine of $1,000 if the person returned after being removed; in still another of the old laws, the Commissioner, with the approval of the Secretary, might remove any person deemed "detrimental to the peace and welfare of the Indians," and this action was not reviewable by the courts.

The web of laws and regulations, not contemplated in the beginning, made of the Indian reservation a veritable prison. They engendered in the public mind the impression that the reservations were "concentration camps" that should be abolished at the earliest moment. So, also, they gave impression that Indians were "wards" and somehow legally incompetent, and that they were second-class citizens.

Even before the findings and the recommendations of the Meriam survey, Indians had been made citizens.[2] This was accomplished by the Act of June 2, 1924, which provided "That all non-citizen Indians born within the territorial limits of the United States be, and they are hereby, declared to be citizens of the United States: provided, that the granting of such citizenship shall not in any manner impair or otherwise affect the right of any Indian to tribal or other property."

The 1924 act, indeed, completed a process that had been operating for some time. It has been estimated that two-thirds of the Indian population of the United States had acquired citizenship prior to that year, through treaty provisions, through statutes granting citizenship to the individuals of specified tribes, land allotments, and other special legislation.

Against this background the Indian Reorganization Act came into being on June 18, 1934, a hundred years after the formal establishment of an Indian Bureau.[3] It came late in the day. Since the enactment of the General Allotment law, Indians had lost 90,000,000 acres of land and at least 200,000 Indians were either landless or were subsisting on inadequate acreage.

The Indians were not a vanishing people, but they had suffered heavy population losses. As late as 1920, the death rate among Indians was just double the national death rate. The great tribes, such as the Iroquois Confederacy, the Siouan tribes of the eastern seaboard, the Powhatan Confederacy, had been reduced to mere remnants or scattered abroad. Still other tribes, the Cherokee, Choctaw, Creek, Chickasaw, and Seminole, had been torn from their roots, transported a thousand miles to an area west

of the Mississippi River. In the far north the Russians, pushing
their trade across from Siberia, destroyed native villages and en-
slaved the inhabitants. The numerous small tribes in California
were almost wholly annihilated within a few years after the discovery of gold.

The Indian Reorganization Act was designed to restore the
wreckage of a hundred years. It was an effort to rethink the objectives of Indian administration. It reasserted the doctrine of
internal tribal sovereignty. Administrative control over Indian
life had been a destructive and self-defeating device, not a solution to Indian problems.

Indian affairs by that time had come to occupy a surprisingly
large share of public attention. The effort of the Pueblo Indians
to save their lands from confiscation was widely publicized by
women's clubs and church groups. The Meriam survey report laid
before the public the appalling situation of the impoverishment
of the Indian people under a system of government control that
seemed helpless to reverse its own directions. A special investigating committee of the Senate Committee on Indian Affairs began a series of hearings in the field which, starting in 1928,
brought into the open and to national attention cases of mal-
administration which inspired news articles and editorials from
one end of the country to the other.

Even before he took office, President-elect Franklin D. Roosevelt, on January 28, 1933, received a petition signed by more than
600 of the country's leading educators, physicians, churchmen,
social workers, attorneys, newspaper editors, scientists, welfare
workers, and ordinary citizens. Among the signers appeared the
names of President Robert M. Hutchins of Chicago University;
George Foster Peabody of Hampton Institute; John A. Ryan,
National Catholic Welfare Conference; Bishop Hugh L. Burleson,
National Council of the Episcopal Church; John R. Haynes, re-
gent, University of California; Franz Boas, Columbia University;
Charles C. Davenport, Carnegie Institution of Washington;
Oswald Garrison Villard, editor of *The Nation;* Roger N. Bald-
win of the American Civil Liberties Union. Their petition read:

In justification of our request, we point out that the Indians are dependent on the United States government and are at its mercy in ways and to an extent true of no other elements in our population. . . . They depend upon the federal government for nearly all of the services—economic, educational, social, and human—which other populations receive through many federal departments, through the state and county governments, through the private welfare agencies, and through their independent actions of organized self help. . . . The government, as trustee, has not been thrifty with the Indians' estate. . . . The system of property administration, not yet reorganized, insures in its very structure the continued shrinkage of Indian lands, with the complete ultimate disinheritance of more than two-thirds of the Indians still holding property under government trust. A comparable dissipation has taken place, and is continuing, with respect to the Indian owned natural resources and the funds derived from their exploitation. . . . So great is the Indian distress in many tribes, and so rapid is the shrinkage of Indian property held in trust by the government, that we do not believe we are exaggerating when we suggest that your administration represents almost a last chance for the Indians. . . . There is required, we venture to suggest, not only an Indian administration of extraordinary determination and technical ability but a reorganization of the government's system of Indian Affairs, including an extensive reconstruction of Indian law.[4]

Extraordinary steps were pursued in advancing the legislation which would be enacted as the Indian Reorganization Act. Hearings were opened in the House Committee on Indian Affairs in February 1934 (the Bill was introduced in the House by Congressman Howard of Nebraska, and on the Senate side by Senator Wheeler of Montana), and simultaneously a copy of the draft, with explanatory memorandum, was sent to all superintendents, tribal councils, and individual Indians. Regional conferences were set up at Rapid City, South Dakota; Santo Domingo, New Mexico; Fort Defiance, Arizona; Salem, Oregon; Phoenix, Arizona, and Riverside, California. In calling these conferences the Indians were advised that "It is of paramount importance that everyone concerned acquaint himself fully with the provisions of this piece of legislation.

"The administration wishes that the Indians shall convene and shall freely present their questions and voice their opinions."

The meetings were held, hurriedly, and not everyone understood the meaning and purposes of the proposed legislation. Many Indians could not believe that their views were actually desired, and they could only conclude that the maneuver was a device to get their consent to measures which would destroy them. Nevertheless, Indian views were expressed and made of record and transmitted to the congressional committees. It was the first time such a procedure had been followed in the long history of Indian legislation.

Moreover, the legislation, as finally adopted, provided that it would not apply on any reservation where a majority of the Indians voted against its application—again an unprecedented procedure. A total of 263 tribes voted on the Indian Reorganization Act, 192 accepting it and 71 rejecting it. The act provided:

1. No lands still in tribal ownership shall be allotted in future. (Since the act was permissive, this provision did not apply to tribes that rejected the act.)

2. An annual authorization of $2,000,000 for the purchase of lands, such purchases to be held under trust and exempt from taxation.

3. Lands that had been withdrawn from tribal ownership for homestead settlement but not entered might be returned to the tribe, at the discretion of the Secretary of the Interior.

4. That conservation practices be adopted with respect to timber, grass, and other natural resources.

5. Authority for a revolving credit fund of $10,000,000 from which loans might be made to tribes incorporated for credit and other purposes.

6. That the Secretary of the Interior assist Indian tribes in adopting written forms of government, to exercise "the inherent powers of Indian tribes" and certain additional specified powers.

7. For loans to Indians for the payment of tuition and other expenses in recognized vocational and trade schools, high schools, and colleges.

8. That the Secretary of the Interior establish standards for

employment, "without regard to civil service laws, to the various positions maintained, now or hereafter, by the Indian office," and that Indians meeting such non-civil service standards "shall hereafter have the preference to the appointment to vacancies in any such positions."

Looked at in closer detail, the legislation, in a real sense, reaffirmed the doctrine of limited sovereignty which, until 1871, had been exercised by the Indian tribes. In order that this principle should not go unexercised, Nathan R. Margold, the solicitor for the Department, caused an investigation to be made of the "inherent" powers of Indian tribes. This resulted in an exhaustive study of all existing treaties and statutes, prosecuted in brilliant fashion by Felix S. Cohen, to determine what municipal powers of the Indian tribes had been specifically limited or terminated.

Congress has plenary power to legislate in the field of Indian affairs and may exercise this power to curtail or eliminate tribal powers; but until and unless Congress does so act, the courts have recognized that the tribes may continue to exercise the powers proper to their status as "domestic dependent nations."

The solicitor's report resulting from this study indicated that Indian tribes possessed the right (1) to determine their form of government, which might follow customary law, or might take written form; (2) to administer justice, the tribal jurisdiction being limited by acts of Congress which had placed ten specified major crimes under the jurisdiction of the federal courts—otherwise, crimes or misdemeanors and civil actions involving one Indian against another in so-called Indian country remained within the jurisdiction of the tribe; (3) to determine tribal membership —in this field, also, Congress had intervened and caused final rolls of memberhip to be made for some tibes, but in the absence of congressional action the general power remains; (4) to regulate inheritance, except that the power has been limited on those reservations where the tribal land was allotted; (5) to levy taxes on tribal members and to levy fees on nonmembers doing business on tribal property; (6) to exercise the usual authority of a landlord, including the right to exclude persons not members of the tribe; (7) to regulate domestic relations, provide for the adoption of children, etc.[5]

From this review of tribal powers, inherent in nature, not derived from the United States, it is apparent that the tribes have a substantial base on which to operate as self-governing units.

In the next few years, 135 constitutions were written and adopted by vote of the tribes. In basic design the tribal constitutions were similar, yet each differed in significant details. Thus, some tribes provided a voice for their traditional chiefs or headmen; one tribe provided that its council should be composed of representatives elected and subject to recall by its ancient villages; another tribe provided for a dual council, one composed of the elder men of the tribe who would control all matters affecting tribal lands and treaties, and the other a kind of business committee to deal with current affairs.

Usually the constitutions included a definition of territory over which the tribal jurisdiction would extend; a provision defining membership and establishing a procedure by which membership might be obtained or relinquished; procedures for organizing a governing body and providing for the manner of calling and conducting elections; an article defining the powers to be exercised by the governing body; rules for the use of tribal lands; authorization for the creation of courts to administer justice; guarantees with respect to civil rights—in short, the powers and procedures that ordinarily would be found in a charter of municipal government.

The Indian Reorganization Act also provided that tribes, after adopting a form of government, might apply to the Secretary of the Interior for a charter of incorporation. Such a charter conveyed the power to own, manage, and dispose of property, within legal limitations. The tribe might not sell or mortgage its own tribal lands, that being one of the matters limited by existing law. A charter, once issued, might not be revoked except by act of Congress.

This legislation, called variously the Wheeler-Howard Act or Indian Reorganization Act, became the cornerstone of Indian affairs administration and continued so for the next fifteen years.

Describing it as the most important piece of Indian legislation since the 1880's, Commissioner John Collier in 1934 commented:

It not only ends the long, painful, futile effort to speed up the normal rate of Indian assimilation by individualizing tribal land and other capital assets, but it also endeavors to provide the means, statutory and financial, to repair as far as possible, the incalculable damage done by the allotment policy and its corollaries. . . . The repair work authorized by Congress under the terms of the Act aims at both the economic and spiritual rehabilitation of the Indian race. Congress and the President recognized that the cumulative loss of land brought about by the allotment system had robbed the Indians in large part of the necessary bases for self-support. They clearly saw that this loss and the companion effort to break up all Indian tribal relations had condemned large numbers of Indians to become chronic recipients of charity; that the system of leasing individualized holdings had created many thousands of petty landlords unfitted to support themselves when their rightful income vanished; that a major proportion of the Red race was, therefore, ruined economically and pauperized spiritually.

In a more generalized statement of his concept of Indian affairs administration, Commissioner Collier wrote in 1938:

Our task is to help Indians meet the myriad of complex, interrelated, mutually dependent situations which develop among them, according to the very best light we can get on those happenings—much as we deal with our own perplexities and opportunities.

We, therefore, define our Indian policy somewhat as follows: So productively to use the monies appropriated by the Congress for Indians, as to enable them, on good, adequate lands of their own, to earn decent livelihoods and lead self-respecting, organized lives in harmony with their own aims and ideals, as an integral part of American life. Under such a policy, the ideal end result will be the ultimate disappearance of any need for government aid or supervision. This will not happen tomorrow; perhaps not in our lifetimes; but with the realization of Indian hope due to the attitudes and actions of this government during the last few years, that aim is a probability, and a real one.

The immediate concentration of the Collier administration was on land acquisition and economic rehabilitation through the use of credit and technical assistance.[6]

The act, as mentioned, authorized an annual appropriation of $2,000,000 for the purchase of land. This total authorization was never appropriated in any one year; but until the advent of World War II, funds were made available each year. Other authorizations and sources of funds were utilized to acquire additional land: the Indian Reorganization Act authorized the restoration to Indian ownership of reservation lands opened to homesteading but never acquired by homesteaders; the resettlement administration in the Department of Agriculture purchased so-called submarginal lands, and some of these lands were transferred to the Department of the Interior for Indian use; various special acts authorized land purchases for specific tribes; many tribes with their own funds embarked upon a land purchase program. Through these various devices, by June 30, 1941, approximately 4,000,000 acres had been added to the Indian land base.

So a start was made, but the program never progressed much beyond that point. The war years came on, cutting off appropriations, and by the end of the war the climate had changed, as we shall see.

The Indian Reorganization Act authorized a revolving credit fund of $10,000,000, later enlarged to $12,000,000. In this case, as in the case of the authorization for land purchases, the full amount was not appropriated. By 1945, about $4,250,000 had been appropriated, and the government had made loans to Indian borrowers in excess of $5,500,000. The repayment record had improved steadily. The loans ran from three to five years and the first repayments were due in 1940–41. Delinquency in the first repayment schedule ran at 7.64 per cent; the following year it decreased to 4.95 per cent; in 1943 it was 3.41 per cent; and in 1944, 2.94 per cent.

Out of almost $12,000,000 which had been loaned and on which payment had become due by June 30, 1948, only $3,627 had been canceled as uncollectible.

With access to low-interest-rate loans (the borrowers paid 3 per cent) there was an encouraging rise in the number of Indians who used the land instead of leasing it out, usually to white men with capital and equipment. In the years following the adoption of the Indian Reorganization Act until roughly the end of World War II, the increase in acreage of crop lands farmed by Indians amounted to 400,000 acres; in the same period Indians took over and operated 7,000,000 acres of grazing land which formerly had been operated under lease to white men.

Access to credit also meant increased ability to purchase equipment and livestock. In 1932 Indians owned 171,000 head of beef cattle and 11,003 head of dairy cattle. Total income from the sale of livestock products in that year was $1,230,000. By 1944, the number of Indian-owned beef cattle had increased to 361,000 head and dairy cattle to 50,700 head, while the income from these sources was over $15,000,000 and livestock products valued at $7,400,000 were consumed at home.

In the Commissioner's annual report for 1948, the significant statement is made that "Since the beginning of agricultural extension work on Indian reservations [in 1930], more than 12,000 families have been completely or partially rehabilitated and are now wholly or nearly self-supporting."

The administrative methods pursued by the Collier administration, apart from the operations directed by the Indian Reorganization Act, are worth noting. The Meriam survey had criticized the Bureau for not sharing its responsibilities with other agencies of government, federal and state, and for failing to use, at least in a consulting capacity, the technically trained people available in such agencies. Even before publication of the report, the Indian Bureau had broken this pattern and had gone to the United States Public Health Service for technical help in organizing the Indian health service. In this manner began the practice by which the Public Health Service continued over the years (indeed until the Bureau program was transferred to the Public Health Service in 1955) to make available the services of a director and other personnel.

This policy was continued and expanded after 1933. Co-operative arrangements were entered into with the Civilian Conservation Corps to provide emergency employment for young Indians, the Department of Agriculture in the development of the Soil

Conservation Service, the Resettlement Administration, the Bureau of American Ethnology (Smithsonian Institution), and later with state agencies and various universities.

In an effort to bring to the planning and operating methods specialized knowledge of the social organization and other cultural factors of the Indian people, a unit of applied anthropology was organized in 1935. The unit was designed primarily to assist with the organization of Indian tribes, but to some extent it was used for general consultation. The instructions to field workers emphasized this:

> The most important single task of the applied anthropology unit is to study the contemporary social organization of each group organizing so that the constitutions drawn up will be based on the actual social life of the group. In this way the constitution will not be merely a piece of paper but will flow into and from the life of the people. . . . A second task is to find out in what ways the contemporary native social organization of each group may be fitted into plans for economic rehabilitation. . . . The goal is not science but co-operation in the practical solution of administrative problems through the social science approach. Although not scientific in aim, the procedure in fact-gathering must be as rigidly scientific as in any scientific study.[7]

The Johnson-O'Malley Act of April 16, 1934, which greatly facilitated the policy of co-operation with other agencies, authorized the Secretary of the Interior to enter into contracts with states or territories for "The education, medical attention, agricultural assistance, and social welfare, including relief of distress, of Indians in such state or territory, through the qualified agencies of such state or territory." By later amendments the authority was enlarged to permit contracts with "any state university, college, or school . . . or any appropriate state or private corporation, agency or institution."[8]

Reorganization of the Indian field service, so strongly emphasized in the Meriam survey, on which a start was made during the Rhodes-Scattergood administration, remained still a problem in 1933. The original draft of the Wheeler-Howard bill would have granted Indian communities broad authority to fill positions in local field offices, to take over and operate functions and services, and even, by popular vote, to request the discontinuance of any separable function or service. In the event a function was assumed by the local community, the Secretary of the Interior was authorized to make a legal transfer to the community, including a transfer of funds originally appropriated for the purpose, lands, buildings, and equipment; and thereafter the community might make annual requests to the Secretary for funds to continue operations.

Such procedures were not acceptable to Congress, and the only part of this section that remained was the provision to allow Indians a preference of employment in the Indian Service.

An attempt was made in July, 1934, to achieve some decentralization of Indian Bureau authority by issuing instructions to superintendents and their staffs defining their rights and responsibilities for local program planning and for local administration. The commissioner's report for that year stated: "Superintendents can function effectively, under the new scheme of operation, only with the assistance of an organized staff and with the cooperation of organized Indian representation. Only through bringing about group thinking and group action can they help the Indians into an intelligible relationship with the various specialized government services within reservation areas, and only by group action can they achieve integration of these services into a rational and functional reservation program."

And the report took note: "At best, any government service confronts a new employee with a bewildering maze of restrictive hurdles; at worst, it stifles initiative, breeds inertia, and serves as a refuge for the mediocre. In the past, and up to the present even, the Indian office has tried to improve its personnel service by creating new activities and adding new personnel with little regard to the fundamentals of organization and administration."

Actually, organizational relationships remained fluid, proceeding on a trial-and-error tactic, until 1941, when the commissioner's staff was divided into five branches: Administration, Planning and Development, Community Services, Indian Resources, and Engineering. Previously, the directors of divisions had reported directly to the Commissioner; under the new arrangement, division and section chiefs reported to a branch head.

Then, in 1946, an act of Congress authorized the Secretary of the Interior and the Commissioner to delegate to subordinate officials powers reposed in them by law.[9]

One other aspect should be included in this review of the period, and that was the considerable and sustained effort to gather information as a basis for program and action. The National Resources Board and the President's Great Plains Committee, which functioned in the period 1934–35, gathered basic data on Indian land resources and needs. Technical and administrative personnel within the Bureau co-operated with these agencies in compiling the data and in drafting emergency and long-term rehabilitation plans.

Later, in 1936, a co-operative agreement was entered into with the Soil Conservation Service, Department of Agriculture, and an experimental grazing unit was set up at Mexican Springs on the Navajo Reservation. Also with the Department of Agriculture, a sheep breeding laboratory was created on the Navajo Reservation for the purpose of developing a breed of sheep adapted to Navajo climatic conditions.

A survey and planning unit known as Technical Cooperation-Bureau of Indian Affairs (TC–BIA) was created to conduct human dependency and physical resource surveys on Indian reservations; and, on the basis of its studies, to prepare plans and programs for erosion control, soil conservation, and proper land use. This unit continued in operation until 1939 and in that time carried out reconnaissance or final surveys on more than fifty reservations.

A further step to obtain plans for reservation programs was taken in 1943, when superintendents and tribal governing officials were instructed to co-operate in the preparation of comprehensive long-range plans. Altogether, sixty-seven such programs were prepared, with budget estimates and annual schedules of work to be completed.

After many years of effort by the Bureau and by citizen organizations, an Indian Claims Commission was created by Act of

August 13, 1946.[10] The need for a special court for the purpose of hearing and adjudicating the claims based upon alleged treaty violations and other causes had been obvious ever since 1863. In that year, as a result of certain tribes taking the side of the Confederate states, Congress barred Indian tribes from bringing actions in the Court of Claims. Thereafter no tribal claim against the United States could be brought into court without a special act of Congress. This resulted in interminable delays and produced a feeling of persecution in the Indians.

The Indian Claims Commission was given broad authority to hear (1) claims in law or equity; (2) tort claims; (3) claims based on fraud, duress, unconscionable consideration, mutual or unilateral mistake; (4) claims based on the taking of lands without payment of the agreed compensation; and (5) claims based upon fair and honorable dealings not recognized by existing rules of law or equity. Review by the Court of Claims, subject to appeal to the Supreme Court of questions of law, was provided.

Against the background of delay and frustration which Indians experienced in their efforts to win their "day in court," it might be supposed that the creation of the Indian Claims Commission would be universally applauded. This has not been so.

In 1956, when the original ten-year term of the Commission was due to expire with only a small part of its task completed, legislation was introduced in Congress to extend the term; and at that point the Department of Justice tried through bold frontal attack and through intermediaries to destroy the basis of most Indian claims against the government. This it proposed to do by amending the Claims Commission Act so as to exclude all claims based on aboriginal rights of occupancy; unless a tribe could support its claim by treaty, statute, or other documentary evidence, the Commission would not be permitted to hear its plea. The Justice Department, which defends the United States against claims cases (not just Indian claims), had offered this argument in an important Indian case (the Otoe and Missouri case) and had lost the argument, first before the Claims Commission, then before the Court of Claims on appeal. What it could not win on merit it was trying to win by a political decision in Congress. It lost that effort as well.

The Commission has also been criticized by misinformed writers, who evidently view all Indian claims as spurious and the Commission as a device for raiding the United States Treasury.

It is worth noting, and may be reassuring to the fretful taxpayer, that of the first 131 cases heard and brought to final judgment, less than 4 per cent of the amount claimed in compensation was allowed. In these cases, the total amount claimed was $926,000,000, and awards amounting to $34,199,912 were allowed. Most cases were dismissed without any award.

Whether any given case is meritorious or not, the granting of the day in court indicates to the Indians, and to the world at large, that the United States is willing to submit its actions to judicial scrutiny.

XII

EDUCATION FOR WHAT?

EDUCATION has always been considered a basic tool in helping
the Indian people accommodate their lives to the world of the
white man.[1] The question was: How educate? By what means?
For what purposes?

In the first years of settlement, Indian young people were
taken into private homes, and placed in day schools and institutions of higher learning. Support for these activities came from
missionary societies, private contributions, and land grants. The
Virginia Company, under whose charter Virginia was settled,
made provision for a grant of £10 in currency for each Indian boy
taken into a colonist's home and given instruction. The more
promising Indian boys were sent back to England for training.

In Massachusetts, John Eliot concerned himself with helping
Indians to learn the ways of Englishmen. With Indians par-
ticipating, he laid out nine self-sustaining Indian communities,
marked off into lots, with intersecting streets, planted fields, and
orchards—the Indians who came to settle were called "praying
Indians." Eleazar Wheelock, a Congregational minister, who
founded Moor's Charity School in Connecticut, concerned himself with the academic training of Indian youngsters. The course
of study included reading, writing, arithmetic, English, Greek,
and Latin. The school operated from 1755 to 1769, the enrollment
ranging as high as 150 Indian youths; and when Wheelock moved
over into New Hampshire to establish Dartmouth College, he
sought out and encouraged Indian students.

As the colonies were breaking with England, the Continental

Congress, as a gesture of friendship, authorized funds to engage the services of a minister and a blacksmith for the Delaware Indians, and also provided funds for maintenance of three Indian students at Dartmouth College.

A common method of providing educational assistance was by treaty stipulation, as in the treaty of December 2, 1794, with the Oneida, Tuscarora, and Stockbridge Indians, and the treaty of 1803 with the Kaskaskia Indians. The terms usually called for teachers, material, and equipment for educational purposes.

Evidently, the first specific appropriation by Congress was the Act of March 30, 1802, allowing $15,000 per annum "to promote civilization among the aborigines." In his first message to Congress in 1817, President Monroe urged that effort be made "to preserve, and civilize the original inhabitants." Two years later Congress acted on the recommendation and authorized an annual appropriation of $10,000. The Act of March 3, 1819, in addition to authorizing this expenditure, provided that "The President may, in every case where he shall judge improvement in the habits and conditions of such Indians practical, and that the means of instruction can be introduced with their own consent, employ capable persons of good moral character to instruct them in the mode of agriculture suited to their situation; and for teaching their children in reading, writing, and arithmetic. . . ."

This act remains the basic authorization for the educational activities carried out by the government in behalf of the Indian people.

It would appear that neither the President nor the Secretary of War, the responsible official, had prepared in advance a program for the expenditure of the congressional appropriation. Accordingly, a circular letter was directed to missionary societies, requesting their assistance in planning the use of the fund, and soon the annual appropriation of $10,000 was apportioned among missionary organizations. Later, as treaty funds became available for education, these were generally paid to the missionary establishments.

Although at various times doubts were expressed whether Indians were educable, it is significant that several Indian tribes, with the help of missionaries and educators, built and supported their own schools. This the Mohawks did as early as 1712 under the influence of the Reverend Thomas Barkley, an Anglican missionary. This school, with one temporary suspension, operated until the end of the Revolution. The Choctaws and Cherokees, before their removal from their original homelands, had instituted common schools, supported with funds obtained from the United States for land cessions. After the removal of these tribes to lands west of the Mississippi, the Cherokees (in 1841) and the Choctaws (in 1842) re-established their schools. A number of states had not yet provided for a system of common schools in 1842.

The Cherokee system, by 1852, included twenty-one elementary schools and two academies, and the enrollment in that year was given as 1,100. The Choctaws had nine schools, of which seven experimented with teaching reading and writing to adults. Teachers were brought from the East to be in charge of advanced academic work, and the course of study included music, astronomy, Latin, botany, algebra, and elocution. The Chickasaw, Creek, and Seminole tribes, other members of the Five Civilized Tribes, followed the example of the Cherokees and Choctaws within a few years and established school systems. In all cases, the schools were tribally supported, and operated without federal supervision until 1906, when the tribal governments of these five tribes were destroyed by an act of Congress.

The manual labor school had its beginnings during the period when the tribes were being moved out of the East and Northeast. Usually they were located in Indian country or at a site convenient to several Indian tribes, and for that reason were agreeable to the Indians. Also, they drew support from the government, which subscribed to the view that it was a waste of effort to provide academic training. Still another aspect of the manual labor school appealed to missionary societies and government alike: the labor of the students decreased the cost of operation.

The first such school was the so-called Choctaw Academy, organized by Colonel Richard M. Johnson in Scott County, Kentucky. Supported by government funds derived from treaty an-

nuities paid in behalf of the Indian youngsters, the academy
operated from 1837 to 1842, when removal of the Shawnee and
other Indians deprived it of clients.

The Methodists followed the Indians west of the Mississippi
and established a manual labor school at Fort Leavenworth,
Kansas, in 1839. This school, and others that came later, offered
religious, academic, and practical instruction. Six hours were
spent daily in the classroom and six at work on farm and shop
detail.

The era of the large off-reservation boarding school started
with the establishment of the United States Indian Training and
Industrial School at Carlisle, Pennsylvania, in 1878. It was followed by schools at Chemawa, Oregon, in 1880; and Genoa, Nebraska; Lawrence, Kansas (Haskell Institute); and Chilocco,
Indian Territory, all in 1884. These schools were modeled on the
manual labor schools, providing part-time instruction and part-
time maintenance labor.

To this basic pattern were added military discipline and the
complete regimentation of the child's waking hours. Moreover,
the schools were dedicated to the ultimate eradication of all
traits of Indian culture. The location of the schools at distances
far removed from the reservations from which children were selected was deliberate policy. Children were often no more than
five or six years old when they arrived at these schools. If the
child could be taken young enough and moved far enough away
from the influences of family and tribe, the odds against his ever
again becoming a part of his environment were considered re-
mote.

Part of the plan of operation was the outing system, by which,
when a student completed his school training, he was placed
with a white family for three years. The government paid the
family $50 a year for the child's medical care and clothing; his
labor was deemed sufficient to compensate for the benefits derived from the home situation.

The teachers at that time were appointed by Indian Service
agents, who in turn were political appointees. Even when the
appointive authority was moved to the Washington office of the

Bureau, teaching positions were still part of the patronage system, and many of the appointees were grossly incompetent.

Prior to 1882 there was no uniform course of instruction and each teacher pursued his own way. The first step toward improvement of school personnel, by using the merit system of appointment, was taken in 1885 by Superintendent of Education Oberly, who later became the United States Civil Service Commissioner and after that Commissioner of Indian Affairs. In 1891, agency superintendents, physicians, matrons, and teachers were brought under the classified civil service.

By 1890, the Bureau was placing Indian children in public schools, reimbursing the school or the school district for the actual increase in cost incurred on account of the Indian students. The practice developed rapidly, accounted for by a corresponding decrease in the use of missionary schools. In 1889, Commissioner Morgan declared his intention of discontinuing all contracts with sectarian schools. The announcement precipitated a controversy which continued until 1897, when Congress declared it to be the settled policy of government thereafter to appropriate no public funds for education in sectarian schools. Public funds were continued, in reduced amounts, until 1901, when they were omitted entirely. The policy was later relaxed to permit the use of tribal funds for sectarian schools, when requested by a tribe. The Supreme Court in 1908 upheld this practice.

No major development of methods or purpose occurred during the period 1890–1930. Annual appropriations for education increased, starting at $100,000 in 1870 and amounting to more than $2,000,000 before the end of the century. The number of Indian schools actually decreased during the period 1900–1926, although school enrollments increased. The total number of Indian schools of all types (government, mission, and private) stood at 307 in 1900, and by 1926 declined to 294. Enrollment in all types of schools for 1900 was 26,451, and of that number only 246 were in public school. By 1926, total enrollment was 69,892, with 24,591 students in government schools and 37,730 in public schools.

As characterized by one writer: "Indian education closely trailed the development of the public school system, with slight relationship to Indian needs. The difficulty lay in the slavish imitation of the white school. The empty, expensive, time-consuming education program for the Indian did not bring to him economic betterment, nor did it destroy his native way of life, as it so woefully intended, because his school followed a sterile path and made only a tip-of-the-wing contact with his tribal experience and his actual reservation surroundings."[2]

Government schools were losing ground, while the preference for day schools was directed at increasing Indian enrollment in public schools, without reference to their suitability to meet Indian needs. The total Indian situation was growing progressively worse, due to a staggering loss of land and the inefficiency of education.

In rather close succession three eruptions of public judgment shook the Bureau of Indian Affairs out of its stodginess and set a train of reform in motion.

The first of these was the report of the Committee of One Hundred, consisting of one hundred public-spirited citizens, who met in Washington in 1923 and issued a report the following year. The report covered the whole field of Indian affairs, but gave particular attention to educational needs. It recommended increased federal appropriations for the appointment of competent personnel, provision of adequate school facilities, increased Indian enrollment in public schools, and scholarships in high schools and colleges for Indian youngsters.[3]

The immediate reaction of the Bureau was to increase Indian public school enrollment and revise its course of study to parallel more nearly the public school curriculum. Day schools on reservations were extended to include six grades, boarding schools to eight grades, and nonreservation boarding schools to high school work. At the time of the report Haskell Institute was the only government school offering work above the eighth grade; by 1925, three other schools were offering high school courses and by 1929 the number was six.

As some educationists pointed out, the extension of grades did not necessarily raise school standards; vocational training was mediocre and the course of study still was not related to Indian needs.

Next in the series of eruptive events was the Meriam survey, already described in its general content. It referred to the task of the Indian service as primarily educational, and it found that neither the service as an entire function nor the schools themselves operated from such a premise.

It reported that the first and foremost need in Indian education was a change in point of view. Through the years the policy had been to remove the Indian child as far as possible from his home environment. A new approach, less concerned with the conventional school system and more with the understanding of human beings, was urged. The report questioned the wisdom of prescribing courses of study and uniform examination questions from an office in Washington, when the need was to develop methods which would be adapted to individual abilities, interests, and goals. This could be best accomplished by employing better-qualified educational personnel.

The report was especially critical of the boarding schools, which still dominated the scene, although for some years the Bureau supposedly was directing its efforts away from the boarding school and toward the use of public schools and local Indian day schools. Nevertheless, more than four-fifths of all Indian children enrolled in government school were attending boarding schools, on and off the reservations.

Arrangements for the care of children in the schools, the survey staff found, were grossly inadequate. The diet was deficient in quantity, quality, and variety; dormitories were crowded; medical services were below standard; too many young children were still being enrolled; the schools were still supported in part by the labor of students, and some of the work performed probably violated state child-labor laws; the work program was not an adequate substitute for vocational training—in fact, the facilities for vocational training were inadequate.

Recognizing that the boarding school provided an essential service for Indian children who lived in areas where there were no schools, particularly no secondary schools, and for orphans and children from broken homes, the report recommended that the emphasis should be on training in health, in family and community life, in productive efficiency, and in the management and use of property and income. Also, the schools should be coordinated with the general educational system of the country, for Indian students who desired to go on with their education.

The Bureau had made increasing use of public schools, until by 1920 the enrollment of Indian students in them exceeded that in the Bureau schools. The report commented on this development, and regarded it as a movement in the direction of the normal transition of Indian ways to white. Significantly, however, the survey staff recognized that Indian children and Indian families often needed more service than the public schools were prepared to render. The staff urged that Indian day schools be increased in number and improved in quality. It further recommended that the Indian day schools be designed as community centers for reaching adult Indians as well as children, and be made an integral part of the reservation program.

The last of the trio of special reports was that issued by the National Advisory Committee on Education in 1931. This committee had been organized in 1929 by the Secretary of the Interior at the direction of the President. The scope of the study undertaken by the committee included all of the indigenous people (the mountain tribes of the Philippines, the Polynesians of American Samoa, and the Chamorros of Guam) for whom the United States had some responsibility.

This committee found that the educational policy of the federal government toward the Indian population of the United States had been a tragic failure. It felt that the government had concentrated too exclusively on its fiduciary role and had not given enough attention to training the Indian to be healthful, economically self-supporting, and competent in caring for his own property. The result of such a policy, the committee found, had pauperized the Indian and left him as helpless in the face of a strange economic civilization as he had been in his first contacts with that civilization.

The recommendations of the National Advisory Committee on

Education, while brief, followed the Meriam survey recommendations in urging the establishment of a planning and development division and the delegation of management to local officials as rapidly as new and trained personnel became available. The proper recruiting, training, and retraining of personnel, the report suggested, were strategic to all improvement in the operations of the Bureau of Indian Affairs.[4]

A start was made on most of these recommendations during the Rhodes-Scattergood administration. As noted elsewhere, appropriations for educational activities increased sharply. Under the direction of W. Carson Ryan, Jr., a nationally known educator, a vigorous program was developed, aimed at breaking down regimentation in the schools and bringing the schoolroom facilities closer to the Indians in their communities. By 1932, day school enrollment had increased by more than 2,000 and the development of the community day school was well on its way. Boarding schools that could not be closed immediately were improved by eliminating the lower grades and the younger children and adding high school grades. Vocational training was improved, work detail was appreciably curtailed, and food and health care was made more adequate.

Public school services were better utilized by increasing tuition payments and by the appointment of field supervisors who reviewed public school performance.

However, the deepening depression of those years, resulting in lower farm prices, unemployment, and general distress, impeded and discouraged reforms.

In 1933, at perhaps the low point of the depression, the plight of the Indians had become so serious that the War Department and the American Red Cross were called upon for emergency relief. The War Department dispatched forty carloads of surplus clothing, mostly left over from World War I, while the Red Cross sent thousands of yards of materials, articles of clothing and 5,000,000 pounds of flour.

Perhaps the heaviest blow to the reforms initiated by the Rhodes-Scattergood administration were the findings of Senator William H. King of Utah. These were findings for which the

Commissioner and his assistant were not responsible, except for certain events falling within their term, but they were identified with the Bureau and its misdeeds. A special subcommittee of the Senate Committee on Indian Affairs in 1928 began investigating the Bureau, and Senator King's disclosures resulted from this investigation.

His charge, already noted, that the Indians had lost nearly 90,000,000 acres of land since 1887 could better have been leveled at Congress itself. In the same way, the disclosure that $500,000,000 of tribal trust funds had been expended during the same period; that this money had been diverted to federal uses, such as the painting of Indian agencies and the purchase of furnishings and trappings for local superintendents, as well as in per capita payments to the Indians—of which nothing remained —this too was properly a charge against Congress, since Congress authorized and appropriated the money.

But neither the economic distress of the times nor publication of the disheartening record of mismanagement of Indian property halted reform; achievement was even greater in the succeeding administration.

One of the conditions of Indian education to which the Meriam survey called attention was the "overageness" of the Indian children in school at the time of the survey, reflecting the failure of the Bureau to get children started in school at the proper age and to hold them in attendance. Many factors necessarily contributed to this situation, but generally it indicated that Indian parents resisted the schools, were not aware of the value of education, and needed the children at home as part of the economy of the family.

Twenty years after the publication of that finding, Acting Commissioner William Zimmerman, Jr., stated (1948): "The situation with regard to 'over-ageness' of Indian children in school has improved greatly since 1928. In that year, the first in which there are comparable data on school retardation, only 19 per cent of all children in Indian schools were at the proper grade for their chronological age or were not more than one year retarded. In 1946, the latest year for which estimates are available,

62 per cent were at their proper grade or not more than one year retarded."

The conclusions were based on findings by Dr. Shailer Peterson of the University of Chicago, who conducted a service-wide testing program on Indian school children. Dr. Peterson made additional findings: (1) Children in the elementary grades were making better academic progress than the children then enrolled in high schools; eighth-grade children appeared to have better command of English than twelfth-graders. (2) Children currently in fourth grade in Indian schools more closely approximated the advancement of rural white children than was true of the Indian children in the upper grades. These indicated that improved teaching methods were overcoming the handicaps children faced who entered school with knowledge only of a native language.[5]

Also, at the time of the Meriam survey, only six Indian service schools were offering high school courses, and none was accredited. Some of the schools were later closed and those that remained were improved to meet state requirements. By 1948, twenty-seven state-accredited four-year high schools were operating. In twelve other schools, ten grades were offered and plans existed to add the final two years to some of these schools.

The improvement of teacher and supervisory personnel, started immediately after the Meriam survey, continued as a basic objective. Normal school graduates with two and three years of training continued to be accepted until about 1938. Then, working with the Civil Service Commission, the Indian Service succeeded in raising the standards to require that all teachers have a four-year bachelor's degree, with eighteen credit hours of professional courses in education. Teachers' salaries were increased until, before World War II, the average exceeded the salaries paid teachers in most rural public schools.

Any lingering doubt of the native ability of the Indian people was removed by studies jointly undertaken by the Bureau and the University of Chicago in comparative intelligence tests of Indian children and white children of a rural area in the Middle West.[6]

Recognizing the language difficulty which distorted the results of many previous efforts at measuring intelligence, the Grace Arthur Point Performance Scale and the Goodenough "Draw-a-Man" tests were used with Hopi, Navajo, Sioux, Papago, and Zuni Indian children. The same tests were used with white school children to furnish comparative scores.

The highest average I.Q.'s of children ages six through eleven were made by Hopi children of Arizona. One group of Hopi children had an average I.Q. of 112 and a second group had 111, both on the Arthur Scale. These two groups measured 111 and 117 on the Goodenough test.

The Middle Western children scored an average I.Q. of 103 on the Arthur test and 101 on the Goodenough.

Pine Ridge Sioux children had a range of from 101 on the Arthur to 114 on the Goodenough. The Zuni children ranged from 100 to 112 on these two tests. Papago children ranged from 100 to 109.

Every Indian group had a higher average on the Goodenough test than the white children.

For the first time it was possible to say, as a matter of objective finding, that Indian children were worth educating.

Meantime, the purposes for which Indian children were to be educated were more sharply defined. Willard W. Beatty, who succeeded Carson Ryan as Director of Indian Education, wrote in 1942: "A school program is only valid when it satisfies the needs of the people being educated." So he undertook to find out what these needs might be.

A field study that continued over a four-year period revealed that Indian young people upon completing their schooling (the investigation was directed at boarding school students) either remained at home or returned there within a short time after graduation. Students who had been trained in vocational courses as a rule did not pursue their trades, but found their way back to their home communities. Hence, it became the policy of the Indian service to make available to Indians every possible opportunity to secure a livelihood through the use of reservation resources. In practice, the Bureau developed a diversified school program, with emphasis on vocational agriculture and the production of marketable craft work. In 1948, the Bureau reported:

"The schools of the Indian service are based on standard educational practices, in that the courses of study are equivalent to or are superior to the courses of study in the states in which the Indian schools are located. While there is this basic conformity, the schools have also been adapted to the needs of each reservation or each area, accordingly as the area is primarily devoted to farming, to grazing operations, or to survival on the Arctic coast."

XIII

DESTROYING THE FUTURE
A. Opening Phase

FOR twenty years following publication of the Meriam survey, a sustained effort was made to translate into humane administrative policies and methods the legal and moral principles which the first Congress of the United States and later the federal courts had enunciated.

That first Congress by the Act of August 7, 1789, as noted above, had asserted the promise of "utmost good faith," and left it to future Congresses to enact "laws founded in justice and humanity."

The courts gave substance to the "good faith" promise by defining the nature of the property right in land which Indians were were entitled to assert. Thus, in *Mitchell v. United States* (1835), "The merits of this case do not make it necessary to enquire whether the Indians within the United States had any other rights of soil or jurisdiction; it is enough to consider as a settled principle, that their right of occupancy is considered as sacred as the fee simple of the whites."[1]

Also, their right of self-government. Thus, *Worcester v. Georgia* (1832), "The charters [of the several English colonies] contained passages showing one of their objects to be the civilization of the Indians, and their conversion to Christianity—objects to be accomplished by conciliatory conduct and good example; not by extermination. . . . Certain it is that our history furnishes no example, from the first settlement of our country, of any attempt . . . to interfere with the internal affairs of the Indians, further than to keep out the agents of foreign powers, who, as traders or otherwise, might seduce them into foreign alliances."

The translation of these principles into action had been the purpose of the reforms in Indian administration and the Indian Reorganization Act. These were belated measures, taken after the Indians had lost heavily in lands and other assets, and after a long period of close supervision and interference in their internal affairs had reduced the tribes to abject dependency.

Viewed in terms of the dichotomy already suggested, the situation of the Indians in law and public policy may be expressed in this manner:

A common intention and purpose runs through the Act of August 7, 1789, the court pronouncements, the Meriam survey, the Indian Reorganization Act, and the educational reforms of the second quarter of the present century. They proceeded from the assumption that the Indian people had certain basic rights in the world which they had discovered and, within their means, had developed; and the further assumption that the Indians were men capable of learning and growing in social skills.

Against this assumption, from the beginning, was the notion that the Indian people were primarily hunters whose rights were ephemeral in nature and must cease to exist as soon as the game animals which subsisted them disappeared. Moreover, according to this view, the Indians were really an inferior human stock which, on the one hand, was bound to disappear before the onslaught of a superior race; and, on the other hand, was not likely to profit from educational efforts and should be satisfied with a modicum of elementary instruction.

These latter views can be charitably excused as reflecting a time when educated people possessed only a superficial knowledge (and that largely intuitive) of society and man and the interrelations between the two. It was possible for James Monroe, in the sincerity of his day, to conclude that "a compulsory process seems to be necessary, to break their habit, and civilize them. . . ." Only the intuitive few in 1816 had yet supposed that the brotherhood of man might include brotherhood with

non-Europeans; that is, pagans or infidels. For such, a little com-
pulsion, if needed, would doubtless be for their own good.

It was quite a different matter when, in 1952, a Commissioner
of Indian Affairs, anticipating that Indians might oppose a proposal he was to make to them, instructed his field employees in
this manner: "I realize that it will not be possible always to obtain Indian cooperation. . . . We must proceed, even though
Indian cooperation may be lacking in certain cases."[2] Dillon S.
Myer, the Commissioner at this time, issued these instructions
either without an awareness of the limitation they might place
upon the rights of the Indian people to decide questions affecting
their property, or he willfully chose the view that the Indians
were still simple hunters whose rights need not be taken too
seriously. In the latter case, he followed in a long line of cynical
men, of whom the most distinguished was Andrew Jackson.

The reforms undertaken in response to the Meriam recommendations, and directed to be taken by the Indian Reorganization Act, did not proceed unopposed. Some criticism stemmed
inevitably from hostility to the Bureau of Indian Affairs itself and,
in its mildest form, was the product of long years of dissatisfaction with bureaucratic methods. The attack led by Senator King
on the budgetary practices of the Bureau, already mentioned, was
of this nature. In part it was justified; in part it was a demonstration of the pot calling the kettle black.

A more ominous kind of attack was one that did not so much
concern itself with pending issues as it used issues, any issues,
in a continuing effort to discredit reform programs and to inspire
opposition to the reasonable aspirations of the Indian people. The
basis of this kind of attack, it would seem, was an unwillingness
to have a halt called to the destructive processes of the half-
century which preceded the Indian Reorganization Act. Whatever motives the attackers might have, the events before 1934
must have comforted them individually, or supported their
private views. The transfer of Indian lands to white ownership
must have had their approval. The denial to Indians of a voice in
the management of their affairs must have seemed proper. Perhaps they had predicted the abolishment of the Indian reserva-

tions at an early date; perhaps they had anticipated an end to tax-exempt Indian trust lands. If one sees Indians as savages, or the often-used euphemism "children," perhaps no other view and no other course of action are possible than to work for their early extermination. Let them make way for progress, as the Cherokees had made way, as Indians always had made way.

The strategy was to attack the appropriations authorized by the Indian Reorganization Act. Economy in government is always popular and attack on the costs of a program need not divulge any other motives.

At the very heart of the Indian problem was the need for land and credit. The Meriam survey had emphasized this; the investigation carried on by the National Resources Board in 1934 had reported the need in great detail; the President's Great Plains Committee in 1935 had emphasized the need within a limited region.

The National Resources Board recommended as "urgently needed," in the Great Plains area alone, the acquisition of 9,700,-000 acres. Urgently needed was defined as "the mere subsistence level above the verge of starvation and the dole." It added the further recommendation that, to raise the Indians above bare subsistence to the living standards of their rural white neighbors, the government should acquire for the Indians 25,500,000 acres at a cost then estimated at just over 100,000,000 dollars. As the Board noted, this was but a fraction of the land area which the Government had allowed to pass out of Indian ownership.[3]

The Indian Reorganization Act authorized an annual appropriation of $2,000,000 for land purchase, but in no year was this entire amount appropriated. From 1935, when the first appropriation was made, until 1950, approximately $5,500,000 was provided, sufficient to acquire about 400,000 acres of land.

Fortunately sources of funds and transfer authorities were available outside of the Indian Reorganization Act, and other lands were added to Indian holdings, as follows: 875,000 acres by special legislation; 1,063,000 acres of public-domain grazing lands designated for exclusive Indians use; 965,000 acres of lands formerly belonging to the Indian tribes and, under the authority of the Indian Reorganization Act, restored to Indian ownership; and finally, Indian tribes, using their own funds, acquired about 390,-000 acres at a cost of over $2,000,000. The total of these acquisitions after fifteen years was less than 4,000,000 acres, not even half the lands "urgently needed" in the Great Plains area alone.

The credit needs of the Indian population were estimated by the National Resources Board in 1934 at $66,000,000, to include funds for capital investment (buildings, improvements, etc.), annual farm operating costs, rehabilitation of unemployed Indians, and co-operative and tribal enterprises. The Indian Reorganization Act authorized a revolving fund of $10,000,000, later increased to $12,000,000. The National Resources Board recommended that the authorization be appropriated in full. By the end of 1948, appropriations amounted to $6,600,000, of which about $1,100,000 represented accumulative administrative costs, leaving a balance of $5,500,000 for loans.

Accomplishment did go forward, even though program funds fell short of promises. As accomplishment grew, opposition increased in tempo and became more direct.

An extreme example of the new attack was a so-called Senate Report 310 released during the 78th Congress (1943). Members of the special investigating subcommittee, in whose name the report was released, protested subsequently that they allowed their names to be used without knowing what was in the report. Nevertheless, the document was never recalled, and there is no reason to believe that the report did not represent the views of some members of the committee. This document called for:

1. The immediate elimination of all research, special studies, surveys, conferences, and all supervisors, directors, co-ordinators, and specialists of every description.

2. Elimination of rehabilitation programs for Indians.

3. The transfer of the management of forests, irrigation works, hospitals, schools, to other agencies, federal or state.

4. Immediate cessation of all land purchases.

5. The division of all trust funds among the individual members of tribes and removal of Indian lands from trust status.

6. The reduction of staff to the absolute minimum needed to close out the affairs of the Bureau of Indian Affairs.

The attack was next directed against efforts being made in the Department of the Interior to determine and validate the rights of the natives of Alaska to the lands they had occupied and used from immemorial time. Some words of explanation will be needed to make this situation clear.

The Indian Reorganization Act did not apply in its entirety to the natives of Alaska, but by amendatory act of May 1, 1936, the provisions of the statute were made applicable.[4] In addition, the amendment authorized the Secretary of the Interior "to designate as an Indian reservation any area of land which has been reserved for the use and occupancy of Indians or Eskimos . . ." by previous law or executive order. In designating such an Indian reservation, the Secretary was authorized to attach additional lands to those previously reserved if the lands added were actually occupied by Indians or Eskimos. No designation as a reservation would be effective until it had been voted upon, by secret ballot, and approved by a majority of the Indian or Eskimo residents.

In 1944, in accordance with this authority, the Secretary designated six Indian reservations in Alaska, and these were approved by the resident natives in duly called elections. In two other cases where such designations had been proclaimed and elections called, the natives by majority vote rejected the designation.

The six approved reservations together totaled a little over 1,500,000 acres, the smallest amounting to 870 acres and the largest 1,408,000 acres. The latter was a hunting reserve north of the Arctic Circle, where the economy of the people was based on fur trapping and moving with the migrating caribou herds.

In requesting these reservations, the Commissioner had written: "The large influx of population into Alaska as a result of war activities, and the growing encroachment of the whites upon the land and resources of the Indians and Eskimos have served to emphasize the most serious problem confronting the natives—the protection of their ancestral hunting, trapping, and fishing bases."[5]

Until the adoption of the Alaska amendment to the Indian Reorganization Act, no machinery had existed and no action had been taken to determine the rights of the natives in the land.

The Treaty of Cession with Russia of 1867 had provided that the native tribes, if they elected to remain in the territory (they had the alternative of maintaining their Russian citizenship by migrating to Russia), would be admitted "to the enjoyment of all the rights, advantages, and immunities of citizens of the United States, and shall be maintained and protected in the free enjoyment of their liberty, property, and religion."

In 1884, in authorizing the formation of a territorial government for Alaska, the Congress had provided "that the Indians or other persons in said district [Alaska] shall not be disturbed in the possession of any lands actually in their use and occupancy or now claimed by them but the terms under which such persons may acquire title to such lands is reserved for future legislation by Congress." The natives were given a similar promise of protection when, in 1891, the homestead law was extended to Alaska: their lands were not to be entered upon for purposes of settlement.

The 1,500,000 acres included in the six reservations, the Interior Secretary pointed out to Congress, amounted to less than one-half of 1 per cent of the land area of the territory. Furthermore, "Practically all these reservations consist of tundra with little vegetation or other resources. The protection of native land rights and resources in areas where natives are practically the only inhabitants, does not retard but insures the development of those areas."

These reasons notwithstanding, there were introduced in the Senate in 1948 a proposed joint resolution to abolish the six reservations, and a proposed bill. The resolution read in part:

Whereas any aboriginal titles which may be claimed to have existed with respect to lands within the territory of Alaska were extinguished under the terms of the treaty of June 20, 1867, between the United States and Russia; and

Whereas the United States never recognized the rights of natives based upon use and occupancy of lands in Alaska, except to the extent that certain individual rights have been recognized in the case of natives in the same manner as in the case of others; and . . .

Whereas the inclusion of vast areas within Indian reservations, and the possibility of inclusion of other lands in such reservations, is retarding the settlement and development of Alaska . . .

The resolution then provided for rescinding the authority of the Secretary to create reservations in future.

In reporting on this resolution, the Acting Comptroller General of the United States wrote to the Senate:

Whether the authority of the Secretary of the Interior to establish Indian reservations in Alaska should be limited or revoked, and whether his orders heretofore promulgated establishing such Indian reservations should be rescinded, are matters of policy with respect to which this office has no recommendations to make. However, for the consideration of your committee, the following comments are made as to claims by the Indians which may be anticipated as a result of rescission of the said orders.

The Indians residing on the said reservations may regard themselves as deprived of a legal right if their reservation lands are restored to the public domain without their consent or compensation to them and may contend that the action of the Congress in restoring the reservation lands to the public domain constitutes a "taking" in the eyes of the law.[6]

The Comptroller General is, in effect, the head accountant for the government, and therefore an official who is sensitive about money claims the United States may have to pay. He felt it his duty to remind Congress that the natives might win if they went to court. He pointed out:

"The case of the *United States* v. *Alcea Band of Tillamooks* decided in 1946, involved a claim for the value of lands in Oregon which were taken by the United States and the claim was based solely on aboriginal Indian title. The Court of Claims awarded the Indians a judgment on that basis . . . and the judgment was affirmed by the Supreme Court."

The resolution was not adopted, and neither was an accompanying bill, S. 2037, by which all functions, services, funds, and authority relating to Indian affairs would have been transferred from the Department of the Interior to the Territory of Alaska.

They failed of passage, but the extensive hearings held in connection with these proposals were an indication of how strong a current was running against the Indian people.

XIV

DESTROYING THE FUTURE
B. Full-Scale Attack

IN THE end, the attacks came to be centered on the entire process of Indian development: on the Indian Reorganization Act itself; on the efforts to enlarge the Indian land base authorized by that act; on the effort to supply low-cost credit to the Indians, in spite of the exceptional repayment record; on the new Indian schools; on the tribal enforcement of law and order within the reservation; on the trust structure, created by treaty and agreement, implemented by statutes, which guaranteed the protection of property; and finally, as in 1887, on the tribe as the embodiment of the Indian will to survive.

It will help to understand the nature and purposes of these latter attacks if certain antecedents are kept in mind.

We go back to an observation found in the Meriam survey report "that a striking lack of development of community life for useful ends was apparent." The survey staff offered the opinion that so long as such a condition existed, no other program of assistance could hope to succeed. The efforts to develop tribal self-government, to release the Indian and his property from oppressive laws and regulations, and to educate for resource and community development all were designed to overcome this basic deficiency. Here are the steps by which that design was carried forward:

The Act of July 1, 1932 (Leavitt Act), authorized the cancellation of debts against Indian land, often incurred without their consent; and postponed the due date on irrigation construction charges so long as land remained in Indian ownership, thus guarding against seizure.[1]

The Pueblo Relief Act of May 31, 1933, prohibited the Secretary from spending the funds of the New Mexico Pueblos "without first obtaining the approval of the governing authorities of the Pueblo affected."[2] This limitation on the Secretary's authority was made general in the Indian Reorganization Act of 1934. All tribes adopting written constitutions were empowered to veto any proposed disposition of tribal assets by a government official.

The Act of May 21, 1934, already mentioned, repealed twelve sections of the United States Code which hampered freedom of speech, empowered the Commissioner of Indian Affairs to remove from an Indian reservation any person deemed "detrimental," and sanctioned military control within reservation boundaries.

The Indian Reorganization Act (see above) gave recognition to the residual inherent powers of Indian tribes, and granted additional powers. For the first time in a long legislative record, Congress permitted one of its own actions to be accepted or rejected by vote of the Indian people.

The charters which tribes adopted under the Indian Reorganization Act provided that after a term of years, ten years in most cases, the tribe might vote to terminate the Secretary's authority to supervise the leasing of tribal lands, the making of timber sales, mineral and other types of land-use contracts, the making of loans to its members, the pledging of income, and related matters of a corporate nature.

The leasing of Indian allotments was first authorized in 1891 and the function was closely supervised by the government. The Indian landowners neither bore the cost of such administration nor shared any responsibility for it. The first reform of this policy is contained in the Act of May 11, 1938.[3] This act provided that tribal governing bodies might execute leases for mining purposes, with the approval of the Secretary; and, as noted above, an incorporated tribe might vote to remove the Secretary's authority.

Control over leasing was further relaxed in 1948 by revised regulations. Tribes were authorized to administer their own leasing enterprises, the costs to be met out of fees; and individual landowners were encouraged to lease their own land and the land of minor children and collect lease rentals directly from the client.[4]

In 1946, again by regulation, reservation superintendents were authorized to issue clear and unrestricted title for chattel goods previously held in trust by the United States. Indian borrowers from the revolving credit fund, for example, were not able to get title to cattle or other property purchased with loan funds, even when the loan had been paid in full, without first obtaining a permit for each animal or piece of property involved. Under the new regulations, borrowers were encouraged to take title in their own names at the time of purchase, the property to become theirs automatically upon payment of the loan.

These were significant steps, and others might be cited, by which a bureaucracy moved to divest itself of the blanketing authority it once exercised and to encourage the Indians to take over management of their affairs.

This purpose was stated in great detail by Commissioner Collier on November 15, 1943, in a circular urging the development of reservation plans. The Commissioner wrote:

I see the broad function of Indian policy and Indian administration to be the development of Indian democracy and equality within the framework of American and world democracy. . . .

The most significant clue to achieving full Indian democracy within and as a part of American democracy, is the continued survival, through all historical change and disaster, of the Indian tribal group, both as a real entity and a legal entity. I suspect the reason we do not always give this fact the recognition it deserves is that we do not want to recognize it. Indian "tribalism" seems to be foreign to our American way of life. It seems to block individual development. We do not know how to deal with it. Consciously or unconsciously, we ignore it or try to eliminate it. Remove the tribe, rehabilitate the individual, and our problem is solved—so runs our instinctive thinking. . . .

We can discard everything else if we wish, and think of the tribe merely as a fact of law. At the minimum, the tribe is a legally recognized holding corporation—a holder of property and a holder of tangible rights granted by treaty or statute, by virtue of which a member enjoys valuable privileges which as a non-member he could not have. Through court decisions—many of them Supreme Court decisions—an important body of legal doctrine has grown up about the concept of the tribal entity. This fact of law is an enormously important, persistent, stubborn, living reality. . . .

Now this fact of law was greatly clarified and strengthened by the Indian Reorganization Act, which converted the tribe from a static to a dynamic concept. Congress, through the Indian Reorganization Act, invoked the tribe as a democratic operational mechanism. It reaffirmed the powers inherent in Indian tribes and set those powers to work for modern community development. In doing so, Congress recognized that most Indians were excluded from local civic government and that no human beings can prosper, or even survive, in a vacuum. If we strip the word tribe of its primitive and atavistic connotations, and consider tribes merely as primary or somewhat localized human groups, we can see that Indian tribal government, for most Indians, is the only presently feasible type of local civic self-government they can share in and use for their advancement. We can divest ourselves of the lingering fear that tribalism is a regression, and we can look upon it as a most important single step in assimilating Indians to modern democratic life. . . .

I cannot predict how long tribal government will endure. I imagine it will be variable in duration. I can imagine some tribes will remain cohesive social units for a very long time; others will more or less rapidly diffuse themselves among the rest of the population. It is not our policy to force this issue. Indians have the right of self-determination. And cultural diversity is by no means inimical to national unity, as the magnificent war effort of the Indians proves. . . .

During this transitional period (however short or long it may prove to be) the federal government is forced both by the fact of law and the fact of self-interest to continue to give a friendly guiding and protective hand to Indian advancement. As to law: there is a large body of treaties and statutes to be interpreted and enforced; Indian property must continue to be protected against unfair practices by the dominant group; Indians must be assisted in attaining self-subsistence and full citizenship. As to government self-interest: the complete withdrawal of this protection would merely substitute a more difficult problem in place of one that is on the way to solution. It would create a permanently dispossessed and impoverished group that will either have to live on the dole or become one more sore spot in the body politic. . . .

The government's relationship to Indians is itself in a transition period. The Indian Reorganization Act made that inevitable. The Indian office is moving from guardian to advisor, from administrator to friend in court. In this transition, many powers hitherto exercised by the Indian service have been transferred to the organized tribes; many more such powers will be transferred. As Indians advance in self-government, they will begin to provide many of their own technical and social services or will depend more and more on the services ordinarily provided to American communities. I think we can agree, however, that federal advisory supervision ought not to be withdrawn until Indians have attained a fair political, economic, and cultural equality.[5]

The circular then urged that planning be accomplished *with* Indians and not *for* Indians; that plans should not be merely accepted but co-operatively devised by the Indians. This meant more than consulting the tribal governing body, and more even than transferring powers to organized tribes. It meant that the people, the small communities within the tribe, should be organized for planning. They should understand their own situations, become conscious of their own needs, acquire knowledge of their resources, and make decisions in terms of their knowledge.

Whatever else the efforts of those years might have accomplished, they did not succeed in taking Indian affairs out of politics. The Republican-controlled 80th Congress had committed itself to a pledge of reducing "big government" and cutting the costs of government. Although the Bureau of Indian Affairs operated on a relatively modest budget within the federal household, no operation went unnoticed in that 80th Congress.

A demand was made upon the then head of the bureau, Acting Commissioner William Zimmerman, Jr., that he inform Congress (in this case, the Senate Civil Service Committee, which conducted the hearing) of what specific reductions of expenditure the Bureau might put in force immediately. When a direct reply was not instantly forthcoming, the Acting Commissioner was subpoenaed by the committee and required to return on the following day with information and supporting documents to show what tribes could be removed at once from government supervision and what amounts of money would be saved for each tribe so removed.

In the subsequent testimony, Mr. Zimmerman attempted to suggest criteria for deciding whether supervision over trust property and withdrawal of federal services could be accomplished without damaging people.[6] The Bureau was aware, as were members of Congress, that some tribes were already paying most of the costs of administration. Federal supervision might be withdrawn from such tribes, under appropriate safeguards, without adverse effect. There were other tribes, not yet in that position, which might be moved along and in a few years be prepared to move out from under trusteeship. A still larger group of tribes, for various reasons (e.g., lack of education, nonuse of the English language, impoverishment), would not arrive at that point for many years.

Lists of tribes under these three categories were prepared; but deciding what tribes should go under which headings, once the obvious choices were made, was like a blindfolded man picking names out of a hat. The answers given to the Senate were tentative, and could not have been otherwise, without time to review the facts about each.

The information supplied to the committee in this manner was used repeatedly in Congress as evidence that the time had come to terminate immediately federal trusteeship for the tribes specified by the Acting Commissioner, and for all others at the earliest possible date. The attempt by the Acting Commissioner to suggest criteria as guides to congressional action was ignored. Before termination should take effect for any tribe, he urged careful study of the following factors: (1) the degree of assimilation of a tribe, as indicating acceptance by the Indians of white habits and acceptance of the Indians by the white community; (2) economic condition of a tribe, to indicate a reasonable possibility of gaining a livelihood through the use of available resources; (3) willingness of the tribe to dispense with federal aid and guidance; and (4) willingness and ability of states and communities to provide public services.

The next major development, leading finally to the policy

which now dominates Indian affairs, was a resolution adopted in the second session of the 82nd Congress (H. Res. 698) on July 1, 1952, directing "a full and complete investigation" of the activities and operations in the Bureau of Indian Affairs.

The House did not provide funds for the investigation after adopting the resolution, and accordingly the chairman of the subcommittee appointed to make the investigation directed a letter to the Commissioner of Indian Affairs asking for a complete report under nine headings, including:

1. The manner in which the Bureau of Indian Affairs had performed its functions of studying the various tribes, bands, and groups of Indians to determine their qualifications for the management of their own affairs without further supervision of the federal government.

4. Names of tribes, bands, or groups of Indians now qualified for full management of their own affairs.

5. The legislative proposals designed to promote the earliest practicable termination of all federal supervision and control over Indian affairs.

8. Recommended legislation for removal of legal disability of Indians by reason of guardianship by the federal government.

In Commissioner Myer's memorandum of August 5, 1952, it became evident that for some time the Bureau had already abandoned programs of constructive Indian development and had been concentrating on programs to withdraw the government from further responsibility in this field.

The memorandum stated:

During the past fiscal year the Bureau has devoted a great deal of effort to the development of withdrawal concepts and policy. Bureau personnel have been encouraged to give increasing emphasis to withdrawal objectives in their work with Indian groups and individuals in program development and effectuation. In the central office, we have established the Division of Program, whose primary responsibilities are to render guidance and assistance to Bureau personnel engaged in withdrawal programming at area and agency levels and to formulate Bureau withdrawal programs in cooperation with other central office staff at national levels. We have reached the stage where it has become desirable to crystallize certain Bureau withdrawal policies, establish methods basic to the development of withdrawal programming, and fix responsibilities for proceeding with the task.

Dissent would not be allowed: "We must proceed, even though Indian cooperation may be lacking in certain cases."

The final step in regression was the adoption on August 1, 1953, of House Concurrent Resolution 108 (83rd Cong., 1st sess.). The essential parts of this resolution read:

Whereas it is the policy of Congress, as rapidly as possible, to make the Indians within the territorial limits of the United States subject to the same laws and entitled to the same privileges and responsibilities as are applicable to other citizens of the United States, to end their status as wards of the United States, and to grant them all of the rights and prerogatives pertaining to American citizenship; and

Whereas the Indians within the territorial limits of the United States should assume their full responsibilities as American citizens: now, therefore, be it

Resolved by the House of Representatives (the Senate concurring), That it is declared to be the sense of Congress that, at the earliest possible time, all the Indian tribes and the individual members thereof (located in four states, and certain specified tribes in addition) should be freed from federal supervision and control and from all disabilities and limitations specially applicable to Indians. . . . It is further declared to be the sense of Congress that the Secretary of the Interior should examine all existing legislation dealing with such Indians, and treaties between the government of the United States and each such tribe, and report to Congress at the earliest practicable date, but not later than January 1, 1954, his recommendations for such legislation as, in his judgment, may be necessary to accomplish the purposes of this Resolution.

This completed the repudiation and abandonment of the considerable twenty-year effort to humanize and bring technical skills to the field of Indian affairs.

The resolution is an inaccurate and wholly misleading statement of the Indian situation. By implying that Indians are not subject to the laws of the United States and may not claim the privileges of citizenship, it brands as unworthy the desire of the

Indian people to retain their tribal identities. By proposing to remove all "disabilities and limitations specially applicable to Indians," it implies that Indians dwell in a twilight zone of perpetual infantilism. One is expected either to view them with contempt for not assuming their rightful obligations as citizens or to pity them as one would the inmates of a walled institution.

The facts do not warrant such uncharitable interpretations.

Indians are full citizens of the United States, having been made so by Congress in 1924. They are subject to its laws, except that when they are within the jurisdiction of the tribe in which they hold membership, they come within the tribe's laws, as other citizens are subject to the local ordinances of the city in which they dwell.

Wardship does not apply to the person of the Indian and, as shown above, it has applied in lessening degree to his property. Wardship was born out of the request of tribes for protection against predatory men, and the United States by treaty and otherwise guaranteed the protection.

Indians do bear the full responsibilities of citizenship. They pay all taxes that other citizens pay, except their trust property is exempt as a condition of the protection in which it is held. Many citizens and organizations enjoy similar exemptions, e.g., owners of certain types of bonds, veterans, homesteads, co-operatives, churches, and educational institutions.

Indians have fought on the side of the United States in all of its wars, even before the prize of citizenship was granted to them.

There are no disabilities or limitations attached to Indian citizenship.

XV

LAW AS THE SOLVENT

REPEATEDLY, in its efforts to resolve baffling problems of social policy, the United States has resorted to the remedy of "passing a law." Various writers have commented on this national habit and have described us as a nation of lawbreakers. The laws that were intended to provide a remedy often had the effect in practice of complicating the original problem—one of the complications being that people became offenders against the law.[1]

The field of Indian affairs is conspicuous for the number and variety of laws enacted for the purpose of bringing about desirable social ends. The statement that some 4,000 to 5,000 laws have been passed in the Indian field may exaggerate the situation, since hundreds of these were private relief acts of temporary and limited application. It remains true, however, that law has often been resorted to as a means of bringing about changes in the habits and customs of the Indian people when effort might better have been directed at the individual and the group where change must take place.

To understand a law, it is necessary often to see it operate in the lives of people. The General Allotment Act was earnestly proposed as the best means of speeding up the process of adjustment of the Indian people. A few were able to hold in mind a view of what would probably happen once that proposal became law. Senator Teller of Colorado saw it. The Indians saw it. But most people who considered the proposal evidently could not see it, and the law was passed.

House Concurrent Resolution 108 is a statement of policy, not of law, but it directed that legislation be enacted to carry out policy. Some of that legislation has been adopted, and one of the resulting acts pertains to the Klamath tribe in the State of Oregon.[2] It was adopted August 13, 1954, in the second session of the 83rd Congress, as Public Law 587.

On the surface, it would seem that if any Indian tribe was in a position to dispense with the trusteeship protection and the social services provided by the federal government, the Klamath tribe was ready in 1954. It was one of the tribes specifically listed in Concurrent Resolution 108. It was one of three tribes (along with the Menominee and Osage) that for some years had been paying all or substantially all of the costs of administering its affairs out of income derived from tribal resources. The only funds spent by the federal government were generally funds that the government normally spends on national programs for such activities as soil and moisture control, road construction and maintenance, and education.

The Klamath is not a large tribe, the membership numbering just over 2,000, of which 379, or less than 15 per cent, are full-blood Indians. All members, according to information prepared by the Bureau for the advice of Congress, are said to be English-speaking.

The Klamath Reservation, located in southern Oregon, consists of just over 1,000,000 acres, on which is located a valuable forest of ponderosa and sugar pine and lesser species. The forest has been harvested under sustained-yield principles since 1913. Income from the forest and other resources amounts to about $2,-000,000 per year. After payment of operating and other expenses, the balance is paid out to the enrolled members of the tribe as a per capita dividend. Each member in recent years has received about $800 annually, and the average family received between $3,000 and $4,000.

If continued as a perpetual-yield operation, the Klamath forest would support the tribal members indefinitely. Evidently this assured income did not stifle the efforts of individuals to increase their earnings by their own efforts. The memorandum of information supplied by the Bureau indicated that 224 families, or about one-third of the 668 families comprising the tribal membership, were self-supporting, having an average annual income of $5,635.

Plans for the ultimate settlement of Klamath tribal affairs had been under discussion for many years. In 1932, a bill was introduced in Congress to incorporate the tribe and transfer to the corporation the management of the forest and other resources, with full authority and responsibility. Some of the basic provisions contained in the original Wheeler-Howard bill were, in fact, included in the Klamath incorporation bill. But at that time Congress was not prepared to consider a tribe-by-tribe transfer of federal responsibility and no action was taken on either the Klamath proposal or a similar bill offered for the Menominee Indians of Wisconsin.

Discussion did not stop at that point. Some members of the tribe continued to urge that it be released from trusteeship, and these members made their views known in congressional hearings. In the 80th Congress (1947) a bill was offered to provide for the liquidation of tribal property and division of the proceeds. Professor Verne F. Ray of the University of Washington, who visited the reservation at that time, reported a deep cleavage within the group, but still a strong majority of the tribe opposed the dismemberment of the tribal property.[3]

The tribal governing body was challenged by one of the Oregon senators to submit to Congress an alternative proposal, since tribal sentiment was so clearly opposed to that offered by Congress. This the tribe did at a meeting held in October, 1947. The alternative proposal would allow voluntary withdrawals from membership in the tribe and payment of the individual's proportionate share. But Congress did not respond to its own challenge.

Meantime, Congress continued to transfer to the tribe more and more of the costs of administering tribal property and social services, but did not transfer commensurate authority. This inevitably increased the dissatisfaction of those members who felt that federal supervision was both expensive and unnecessary. They were getting nothing for their money.

The committees of Congress which held hearings on the bill

that was to become Public Law 587 were obviously impressed by the testimony put forth by the proponents of termination. The Secretary of the Interior was so impressed and so anxious to have those views presented that he went to the extraordinary length of authorizing payment out of tribal funds for the travel expenses to Washington of a witness who was not authorized by the tribe to speak for it. The two authorized delegates were under instructions of the Tribal Business Committee to oppose termination legislation. When the chairman of the tribal committee protested, the Secretary admitted error and promised not to repeat the practice—a promise that he violated soon afterward.

The Indian committees in House and Senate were determined in that 83rd Congress to activate the policy established by Concurrent Resolution 108. They saw trusteeship as a failure; it had not provided a method by which the United States might bring its responsibilities to an end; it had not even earned the United States a good name for its efforts. It seemed likely to some members, and most clearly to the chairman of the Senate Committee (Watkins of Utah), that, if left to themselves, the Indians might postpone indefinitely the time when they would be willing to excuse the United States and agree to go their own way. Congress, therefore, would have to act in what it considered to be the best interests of the Indians.

So it was that, at Klamath, the old question was up for consideration once more, and the test was whether in our own time it would receive any better answer than had been given in the past.

Was morality in the handling of Indian affairs a simple matter of time interval? Were Indian rights in land or other things of value good up to a certain point in time, and worthless after that? Was President Monroe's prescription of a "compulsory process" still the best answer the Indians could expect?

The spokesman for the Klamath people, Boyd Jackson, made a strong plea for an extension of the moral right of the tribe to continue its existence.

Appearing before the Senate committee on February 23, 1954, Mr. Jackson recalled that a subcommittee had spent some days on the Klamath Reservation in 1947, holding hearings and traveling over the reservation to investigate its resources.

MR. JACKSON: Mr. Chairman, you were present, and you were the chairman of that committee, and as I recall you asked how long I thought it would take for us to get to that point that we had in mind. And I think that the record will bear me out that I said, "From fifteen to twenty years." That was in 1947. Several years have gone by. And during the interim period, I don't think that we have been idly sitting by twiddling our thumbs.

We had moved in a direction of eventually meeting the termination by (1) asking that you pass a law transferring the activities of our law and order over to the state. The state has accepted, we are operating under that now.

And (2) the other matter was we asked that the federal law affecting Indians be repealed. That is one step further . . . where we might do some thinking on our own.

We now have before the Congress a bill to set up a lending agency under the laws of our state, which was passed by the House during the first session of this Congress. And that proposes to set up a lending agency with a capital of $1,100,000.

We have also taken care of our relief cases and contributed considerably toward our health problem. That is something we are still working on, hoping to reach some plan that would work. . . .

Now, with these activities having been exercised, and some in process, some actually done, we think that we should be considered to the extent of being granted additional time.

I have spent considerable time with the governor of our state and the members of his staff in discussing this very thing, on the principle that this is an entirely new departure, not only on the part of ourselves, the Indians, but the state and federal government as well. . . .

We want to remain as a going concern, on the same basis as other going concerns operate. But we are faced with problems that other organizations are faced with, that we have no idea, or the least conception of, from the standpoint of a going organization. . . .

And we feel that in order to get to that point in an orderly manner we should be given some latitude, some leeway, or the government itself might set up what they are proposing to do in the form of a reorganization, giving us a charter, or setting up the trustees that they have in mind. . . .

We are not saying that we are just not going to do these things. The state, in my discussion with some of the members, takes the position that they, too, would need a period of education if they are going to support any plan that would be the means of us operating as a unit. They also would have to be educated. . . .

The thought occurs to me: Why should we at this moment get in a hurry? What have we done? What do the Klamath Indians owe to this federal government? We pay our own way as we go along. . . . Why, then, can't the secretary sit down and work out an operating plan that would be spelled out in the law, which would be agreeable to us, which we are willing to sit down and work out with them?[4]

At another point the delegate remarked: "Now, maybe we are overly anxious at this point now. Because it has to do with the last thing that we have got, we cannot be any too careful."

The appeal did not divert the "compulsory process," and in the summer of 1954 the Klamath Termination Bill became law.

By this enactment, the tribe was allowed a period of six months within which to complete a final roster of membership. The Secretary of the Interior could step in and prepare this roll himself if the tribe failed to comply.

Tribal property which had been owned by the members of the tribe in common was vested in the individual members, and the proportionate share of each member became personal property.

The tribe was allowed eighteen months in which to engage the services of qualified specialists for the purpose of studying the resources and making recommendations to the tribe as to how best to manage the resources. Thereafter, the tribe had an additional six months in which to submit plans to the secretary.

Federal trusteeship over tribal property would terminate within three years after the passage of the act. Within that three-year period, the members of the tribe must (1) either transfer its property to a corporation or to one or more trustees, subject in either case to approval by the Secretary of the Interior; or (2) upon failure or refusal of the tribe to complete action within the three-year period, the Secretary would transfer the property to one or more trustees for the purpose of liquidating and distributing the assets among the members.

All personal property and funds held in trust for individuals would be released from the trust within three years.

After distribution, property would be subject to federal and state taxes.

The responsibility which Congress imposed on the Klamath Indians was truly formidable. A tentative estimate of the value of the tribal estate was in excess of $100,000,000. The question they had to decide was whether to create a management corporation or trusteeship, in the hope that they would obtain benefits at least equivalent to those they had always known, or, alternatively, settle for immediate liquidation and quick cash. For many families, this would amount to a quarter of a million dollars.

How able and prepared were the people to make the decisions required of them? It was the judgment of the Department of the Interior and of Congress that the Klamath Indians were competent to decide.

Among the specialists called in to investigate conditions and advise the tribe was the Stanford University Research Institute. Its report issued in the summer of 1956 confirmed a growing opinion among Oregonians that termination could spell disaster for the Indians and for the state.

The institute found only fourteen out of one hundred Indians interviewed who believed that the tribe had requested the legislation. Only six believed that the Klamaths had been selected for termination because their tribe was more advanced than others.

The educational level of the tribe was low. Of one hundred adults interviewed, thirty-nine had grammar school training or no schooling; a smaller number had spent one or more years in high school. Few skilled workmen and no professional people were found.

When asked what they would do with their share of the tribal assets, the sample group admitted no plans had been made. When asked what they thought their neighbors might do, the replies were: "Go on a binge," "drink it up," "gamble it away."

The tribal council chairman, Seldon Kirk, expressed what must have been the views of many tribal members when he remarked: "Us Indians are not ready to take over our estate for the simple reason that we cannot get along together. I expect to see the white man get our lands. We fight among ourselves in the tribal council. We set up committees and they won't work. If a man has enough children he is demoralized by per capita payments and lays around. I think the Secretary wants the white man to get our land."

The timber industry in the Northwest was already in a declining market. A sudden liquidation sale of more than 4,000,000,000 board feet of tribal timber and 250,000,000 board feet of timber standing on individual allotments meant economic disaster. A few years earlier, when voluntary withdrawal of individual members was proposed, it was understood that only a small minority of the Klamath Indians would elect to be paid in cash.

These could have been accommodated by limited sales of timber or other assets, offered in a manner not to disturb the market. Local opinion favored the proposal.

The *Portland Oregonian,* one of the most widely circulated newspapers in the Northwest, had advocated the removal of federal supervision. But as the potential consequences of the Klamath legislation became obvious, the *Oregonian* joined others in urging amendments. "We foresee a time when Klamath County's public welfare lists would be burdened with destitute Indians," the paper warned.

Church groups and citizen organizations were concerned over the manner in which the legislation had been adopted; they were disturbed over an apparent failure to acquaint the Indians more fully with the terms of the legislation and to take adequate measures to obtain their views.

The three management specialists appointed by the Secretary of the Interior to conduct the appraisal of tribal assets and to advise the Indians concluded that the terms of the act could not be carried out in a manner to benefit them. Two members resigned before negotiations were completed.

In the summer of 1956, even members of Congress realized that the time allowed for the several phases of action was all too short —as the official tribal delegates had contended. By that summer, the tribe was required to submit its decision as to the course it chose.

At the last moment, an amendment was adopted in Congress, allowing a "breathing spell" within which amendments to the law might be prepared and acted upon.

The extension of time expired in the spring of 1958. The tribal members, by individual ballot, then had to decide whether to withdraw and take cash or to transfer the assets to a management corporation or trustees.

By that time the appraisal of tribal assets had been completed and published; the value was placed at $121,659,618. This was based on the expectation of what the properties might bring if sold over a two-year period, as required by the law. The pro rata share of each member of the Klamath tribe was worth about $59,000.[5]

When the tribal ballots were counted, 77 per cent had elected to withdraw from the tribe and receive cash. Less than 5 per cent expressed a choice of remaining in the tribe and operating the property as a corporation. Almost 20 per cent expressed no choice —either the ballots had not reached them or the alternatives left them groping for enlightenment. The Secretary decided that the unanswered ballots would be counted with those who chose not to withdraw.

The unexpectedly large percentage of those who chose withdrawal produced a startling reaction. To realize sufficient cash to pay out these individual members, 3,500,000,000 board feet of pine timber and 1,400,000 million cords of pulpwood would be offered in an already depressed lumber market in less than two years.

Obviously, Congress would have to retreat farther in its efforts to solve the problems of the Klamath Indians by legislation. An amendment introduced early in the year was adopted in the closing days of the 85th Congress. The amendment provided that the forest would first be offered to private buyers at no less than its appraised market value. The purchaser must agree to cut the forest on a sustained-yield basis for at least seventy-five years. If the lands offered for sale were not taken by private buyers by

January 1, 1960, the federal government would take over and pay for all or any part of the unsold units that the Secretary of Agriculture deemed suitable for administration as part of the national forest system, but authorization for government purchase was limited at $90,000,000.

The adoption of this amendment may have saved the economy of the Pacific Northwest, but it left the Klamath people in peril.

XVI

THE DISPOSSESSED

THE Relocation Program of the Bureau of Indian Affairs does not come as a new idea in administrative policy; what is new is the emphasis placed on the program. Indians express doubts as to the true purposes of this activity and misgivings as to what may be the unintended results.

Coming as it does at the very time Congress has set for itself the goal of withdrawing federal responsibility from Indian property, the emphasis on moving Indians into urban areas raises questions in their minds. Are they to be moved off their lands to give somebody else a chance to profit from them? Official denial of any such intention does not allay doubt. Indians have been damaged before by good intentions that went bad—as men have been killed by "unloaded" revolvers.

The question is raised whether the emphasis on relocation may not turn attention away, and divert federal funds, from the resource and human development projects that are needed in every Indian community. The funds designated by Congress for relocation purposes have increased in skyrocket fashion, at the very time that termination bills were being pushed in Congress, with no notable increases of appropriations for resource development.

The condition with which the relocation program is designed to deal is well understood by Indians and the specialists who have studied Indian affairs. This is the problem of inadequate resources, the low stage of development of those resources, and the lack of employment opportunities on the reservations or surrounding areas.

The first attempt to deal with the problem seems to have been authorized in a deficiency appropriation act of 1931 which made it possible to establish employment centers at Kansas City, Minneapolis, Los Angeles, Salt Lake City, Phoenix, Riverside and Berkeley in California, and San Carlos in Arizona. In that first year the Commissioner reported that 3,318 Indians were placed in jobs, of whom two-thirds were temporary placements. This employment service continued until the establishment of the various work relief agencies created jobs in the Indian communities.[1]

Human dependency studies of Indian reservations, starting in the 1930's and covering at least all the major reservations, made clear the serious discrepancy which existed between resources and Indian population. The National Resources Board, in the study already mentioned, reported: "Though several of the tribes have land which, if properly used, would be ample, and in some cases more than ample, to support them in a fair degree of comfort, the investigations . . . have demonstrated that even with efficient use of the available land resources, the majority of the tribes show a real deficiency." The Board recommended that these deficiencies be overcome by an adequate land purchase program.

Others who studied the problem, taking account of the fact that a good number of Indians might prefer not to make a living on the land, urged the necessity of training Indians and assisting them to find industrial employment. The experiences of Indians in World War II, when an estimated 40,000 Indians went into war work in heavy industry and others into seasonal farm employment, opened an inviting prospect of future employment. It had been demonstrated that Indians were willing to leave their reservation homes, that they learned industrial skills when the opportunity opened to them, and that they seemed to make reasonably good adjustments in wartime communities. The 25,000 Indians who went into the various branches of the armed services also had an opportunity to learn and perhaps acquire a taste for the world that lay beyond the reservation. Certainly the G.I.'s, it was thought, would lead an exodus away from the reservations

and, by their going and inducing others to follow, relieve the load
that the reservation resources were expected to carry.

But the Indians came back from their war jobs and their military experiences. Not all of them came back; and of those who
returned, many discovered that their livelihood lay elsewhere. No
figures are available, but it seems safe to assume that a substantial
percentage of the Indians who worked in war jobs and served in
the armed forces were back at home within a few months or years
of V-J Day.

The relocation program as it now operates in the Bureau was
started by Dillon Myer soon after he took office in 1950. As director of the War Relocation Authority which operated the camps
in which persons of Japanese ancestry were interned during the
war, he had succeeded in returning masses of people to employment and useful community life, moving them to all parts of the
United States. The methods he used in bringing about resettlement of the Japanese were forceful, and at times coercive. Some
critics of Mr. Myer's Indian policies accused him of transferring
to the Indian situation the same thinking, if not the same
methods, that had served in moving people out of the Japanese
relocation camps.

Mr. Myer denied such accusations and insisted that his was a
more realistic appraisal of Indian needs and aspirations than that
of the men who had preceded him in recent years. He found that:

Over the years governmental programs for the Indians have nearly
always been framed in terms of basic lands resources, and have had
the effect of tieing the Indians to the land perhaps more closely than
any other segment of our population. The government has tried in
various ways to encourage the Indians to make productive use of their
land resources and to acquire basic skills in agriculture, forestry, and
other phases of land management. . . . However, there are and
always have been large numbers of the Indians who have no desire to
be farmers or stock men and who would much prefer some other type
of activity. Yet the ties holding the Indian to the land have been such
that we have not had the kind of movement of the surplus populaion
away from Indian areas that we have had over the past fifty years or
so in most other rural areas of the United States. . . . In far too many

areas we find that the Indians are making no productive use of the lands but are leasing them to non-Indian operators and subsisting at a meagre level on the rental incomes.[2]

This appraisal was realistic, but it introduced no factors that had not been known for some time. Regulations that had grown up out of trusteeship and out of the inflexible requirements of the allotment law placed many barriers in the way of land use and management. This had been realized and considerable effort had gone into relaxing these regulations and the requirements of the law.

It was also true that Indians were not making as full use of the available land as their own need indicated they should. They required credit for this, in order to acquire livestock and equipment; but the volume of credit estimated in 1935 was never made available, even though Indians made excellent use of credit funds advanced to them.

Possibly a more serious deficiency, accounting for the failure of Indians to make full use of available land, was the lack of adequately trained agriculture extension personnel. The director of extension for the Bureau called attention to the nature of this problem in 1938:

When a white extension worker deals with white rural groups he can often get cooperation for a good program within two or three weeks. He is speaking to people who have his own ambitions and whose fundamental reactions to life, often, are his own. When he tries to make effective an equal plan for Indian people, it is another story. Nearly three hundred years of deeply rooted distrust, and an attitude toward life which does not regard the piling up of material means as a first consideration, or of bulwarks against the future as a major significance, make an extension worker's Indian task much more complicated. What he can do with a white group in two weeks may, for these reasons, take him a year or even more, with an Indian group.[3]

The relocation program was an attempt to find an easier and quicker answer to the very difficult and complex problem of, on the one hand, trying to win support in Congress for a renewed and expanded program of land purchase, and, on the other hand, of trying to change in slow and unspectacular ways the habits and attitudes of a people. If the dispossessed and the unregenerated in the Indian population could be moved away, out of sight, the problem would be simplified. In spite of Mr. Myer's insistence that the relocation program was no part of the withdrawal program simultaneously being pushed in Congress, the two fitted like hand in glove.

How has the relocation program worked?

In 1951 when the program got under way, the only assistance given the job seeker was transportation to the city and subsistence until the first pay check. Usually one or more job opportunities were available, and in some cases an Indian had actually been accepted by an employer before he arrived in the city. After the subsistence allowance came to an end, the Indian was on his own. If he found the job unsatisfactory or for other reasons left it, or was fired, he might find it difficult to get further assistance, depending on the circumstances. The program at the beginning had a modest appropriation of $300,000 and did not offer much leeway.[4]

Later the program aids were expanded to include transportation for all members of the family from the reservation to the city; $50 for shipment of household goods; subsistence expenses en route; subsistence expenses at destination for four weeks, and supplemental subsistence in case the relocated worker lost his job through no fault of his own; and grants of up to $50 per person for tools and equipment.

By 1957, the appropriation had been jumped to $3,500,000, and subsistence grants included, over and above those previously allowed, (1) funds for the purchase of medical and hospital insurance for one year for the relocated worker and his dependents; (2) up to $50 per family for clothing and personal items; (3) a similar amount for the purchase of household wares and equipment; (4) up to $250 per family for furniture; (5) tuition costs for one year in vocational or academic courses; and (6) a limited program to assist one hundred families to purchase city homes on a matching-fund basis.

The experiences of the Indians moving from rural reservation communities into industrialized urban areas have ranged from tragic failure, resulting often in the complete disorganization of individuals and families, to cases of gratifying success in terms of increased earning power and apparent adjustment. Figures on the number of Indians who have abandoned the effort and moved on to something else are hard to get, and probably those that have been published are to be taken as approximations. The Indian Bureau reported that for 1953, of the persons relocated through the Bureau program, 32 per cent had returned to the reservation. In 1954, 28 per cent returned; and in 1955, 24 per cent. The practice, however, is for the relocation field employee to keep in contact with the relocated person only until the person has exhausted the forms of assistance to which he is entitled. Records are not kept after that, and it is only by chance that the whereabouts of the worker becomes known to the field employee.

A serious and painstaking effort was made by the Community Welfare Council of Minneapolis to discover what happened to the Indian families who came to that city. The report issued by the council, *The Minnesota Indian in Minneapolis*, in April, 1956, presents some startling and discouraging aspects of the effort to move Indians into the cities.

An estimated 7,000 Indians lived in Minneapolis, most of them coming from nearby Chippewa reservations. The report does not indicate how many were brought to the city through the Bureau's relocation program, but it is known that Indians have moved in and out of Minneapolis for many years as employment opportunities beckoned or faded. The findings of the Community Welfare Council are therefore a general commentary on the problems of Indians coming into an urban area, not a specific study of the experiences of Indians relocated by the Bureau. The problems are the same, regardless of the auspices under which the Indian makes the move. An institutional program can help in easing out the rough spots; it cannot remake the individual who is overwhelmed by the experience. The findings of the Welfare Council are therefore pertinent.

Police records revealed that nearly 900 Indian men were jailed in the Minneapolis workhouse in 1955. Half of the total admissions of women to the Minneapolis workhouse were Indian women. The Welfare Council reported that within a test period of thirteen days, 450 cases were heard in the police court, and of these seventy-two were Indians, including twenty Indian women. All but two or three were charged with drunkenness.

The police judge commented: "Most of those appearing during the thirteen-day period had prior records and some had very long prior records. Due to failure over the years to get any response, and due to their mistrust of us, it has been very difficult to work with the Indians through our probation office, although we have tried many times. As a consequence most of these offenders end up in the workhouse. It is the feeling of the court that over a long period of time the percentage of Indians appearing in the police court will run from 14 per cent to 20 per cent."

The Minneapolis schools reported difficulties with the children of Indian families. In some cases the families were reluctant to enroll their children in school after they arrived in the city. Indian newcomers to the city moved in with families already resident there, and the schools found it difficult to secure an adequate census.

The Indian families were reported to be negligent in following up on the attendance of their children in schools. The suspicion or shyness of the children made it difficult for the teachers to communicate with them. Also teachers found it difficult to discuss the children with the Indian mothers. The children often lacked proper clothing and this sometimes kept them out of school.

The Indian families, with their children, were often employed in the fall or early spring in migrant labor, and school attendance was disrupted.

The schools attempted to meet some of these problems by getting clothing from the Department of Public Relief, by giving special training to teachers with Indian children in their classes, and by trying to work with Indian organizations to correct some of the problems.

Employers in the city did not discriminate generally against the employment of Indians, and employment agencies reported no difficulty in placing Indian job seekers. However, few Indians possessed skills and professional abilities, and they could be placed only in the lower-paying jobs. In one group of fifteen Indians to which the Urban League gave help, there were one skilled worker, four semiskilled, and the remainder unskilled. The Minneapolis Fair Practices Commission indicated that it had no complaints during 1956 from Indians on account of employment discrimination against them.

Arrival in the city, according to the Community Welfare Council report, seemed to be a time of great stress for the average Indian family. Often they were poorly dressed, had no money to tide them over, and moved in with families living in already crowded quarters. They did not know what kind of jobs they could qualify for; neither did they know where to apply for employment or how to fill out employment forms. They did not know how to conduct themselves in an employment interview, and for this reason they often did not apply directly to an employer but tried to secure information through their friends as to where they might be accepted.

The Minneapolis Health Department, while finding it difficult to obtain reliable vital statistics on the Indians, noted that "the average age for death of resident Indians in Minneapolis in 1955 was thirty-seven years, compared with forty-six years for all Indians in Minnesota that year, and sixty-eight for Minneapolis residents."

Housing conditions among the Minneapolis Indians were especially deplorable. The report found that "One Indian family of five or six, living in two rooms, will take in relatives and friends who come from the reservation seeking jobs until perhaps fifteen people will be crowded into the space. In one case sixteen people, of all ages including infants, were found in one unventilated attic room with no furnishings but the electric plate, and blankets and clothing. Indians have been found sleeping in hallways, and in bathrooms. One member of the group had advanced tuberculosis. . . . Under one notorious apartment building which every agency knows, the tenants used to go in through the back door, under the furnace pipes to a room carved out under ground. It had one light, the tenants had to go outside and upstairs to a common toilet."

The report offered suggestions of what might be done: "Perhaps the chief cause for all this misery and waste is that we make no adequate preparation for relocation of the Indians from the reservations. We offer little or no help or guidance to people completely inexperienced in urban and modern living."

Commissioner Myer had noted that, in spite of the considerable effort of the government to encourage Indians to make productive use of their land and to acquire basic skills in agriculture, too many were not using the land but were leasing it instead. The Bureau's statistics bear out the correctness of Mr. Myer's observations. What he failed to note was that the government had made a lesser effort to prepare Indians for urban life. This kind of deficiency cannot be remedied at the eleventh hour by providing an Indian client with tuition payments for a vocational training course as he goes off to the city. More is involved than the acquisition of a vocational skill.

A statement issued in 1955 jointly by Professor Sol Tax of the University of Chicago, Arthur Hillman of Roosevelt University, and John Willard of the American Friends Service Committee in Chicago offers insight and perhaps guidance to those who are concerned with the industrialization of the Indian people:

There are no grounds in history to assume that the disappearance of Indian communities is inevitable. Thus the Indian problem has two distinct dimensions: the freedom of individuals to come and go must be preserved and the opportunities to do so extended; and conditions which facilitate the adaptive self-direction of Indian communities must, in the best American tradition, be created. . . .

It is generally recognized that migration to the city creates opportunities for steady employment and improved material conditions. But beyond that, urban living is popularly seen as a means by which Indian individuals can break away from their traditions and their communities. Potentially, urban living is equally a means of enriching the lives of the Indian communities themselves.

The reservation Indians who come to the city and stay a few months, or remain permanently, and who learn of life here and relay their experiences to others, may well turn out to be the first really important channel of communication bridging the barriers of cultural differences between the Indian communities and the general American society. But the isolating effects of cultural differences are not necessarily overcome by the mere fact of migration to the city.

If the emphasis of relocation could be shifted away from permanent resettlement and placed instead on the adult education opportunities offered by industrial employment, the program would serve a better purpose. The one-way ticket into the unknown is not calculated to appeal to many Indians who could best profit from a period of experience in the urban surroundings. The appeal is often to those individuals in the Indian community who have not done well, who are looking for escape, who may never be able to adjust to any set of conditions.

If return transportation should be made available after a minimum period, possibly a year, and a satisfactory work record, the cost to the government would be less than the cost of operating classes in adult education for the same individual. The experience would convey what no formal instruction could impart: familiarity with new modes of life.

As an investment in the development of the individual, the cost would be moderate. But as that individual returned to the community with knowledge of how other people live and participate as citizens in the affairs of the nation, the benefits to the Indian community would be incalculable. The long-run result might well be, not only better communities, but a growing number of Indians who would choose urban life and would approach the change with less vulnerable expectations.

XVII

THE SENSE OF CONGRESS

A POLICY must be tested by the actions and decisions which rise from it. The Indian Reorganization Act, through its legal authorities as well as through complementary administrative discretion, released a broad attack upon poverty, educational backwardness, health service deficiencies, bureaucratic controls, and dependency.

The policy of withdrawal stated in Concurrent Resolution 108 has also operated through legal devices and through administrative determinations. The Klamath Termination Act is one of the devices. The relocation program, though it was not specified in the resolution, is a mechanism operating administratively for the same purpose. It was frankly proposed to be used for that purpose in a bill to terminate federal responsibility for the Turtle Mountain Band of Chippewa Indians of North Dakota.[1]

The Klamath tribe was to be released from government trusteeship because it possessed abundant resources and could be freed from the government's protecting arm without inconvenience to the people affected, or so it was argued. The very opposite situation prevailed in the case of the Turtle Mountain Indians, and yet termination was proposed for them also.

The reservation is in north central North Dakota, lying along the Canadian border. The group represents the westernmost extension of the large Chippewa tribe, whose territory in historic times included much of the country in northern Minnesota and north of the Great Lakes.

The Turtle Mountain Band relinquished to the United States

158

approximately 10,000,000 acres in northern North Dakota (part
of today's great wheat belt) at a price of 10 cents an acre; and
in 1882, by executive order, a reservation consisting of about
twenty townships, or almost 460,000 acres, was established for
their benefit. Two years later, again by executive order, this
reservation was reduced to two townships.

These two townships were given out in individual allotments,
and proved so inadequate that 2,700 members of the band were
allowed to take allotments on the public domain scattered over
North Dakota, South Dakota, and Montana.

A special appropriation was obtained in 1940 to initiate a land
purchase program, but after 35,000 acres were acquired the program was discontinued for lack of funds. Because of the scattered
nature of the public domain allotments and the inclination of
the group to stay together, and even more because of economic
necessity, a majority of those who received such allotments obtained fee patents and sold the land. Thus, of approximately
400,000 acres given out in public domain allotments, only 128,400
acres remained by 1954.

The 27,000 acres which had been allotted within the two-town-
ship reservation were involved in the usual heirship complications and very little of it remained in economic units. The
population, meantime, had increased from about 3,000 in 1910
to 8,928 in 1954. The total earned income of the entire group at
that time was $21,500, according to information supplied by local
officials of the Bureau of Indian Affairs. Total tribal assets, if sold
and the proceeds divided, would yield a per capita share of $37.

About half the population resided on or immediately adjacent
to the reservation, which is hilly, covered with scrub brush, most
of it unsuited for agriculture. The people are entirely dependent
on seasonal employment away from home in agriculture, railroad
work, and construction jobs.

The information supplied to Congress by the Secretary of the
Interior indicated that "Dependence on welfare assistance of the
various categories is great at Turtle Mountain. Almost five hundred families receive total or partial welfare support at some
time during the year. Because of inadequate employment op-

portunities in the general area, during the winter months there
is a heavy case load of employable persons receiving general assistance. It is unfortunate that continuing welfare support is
looked upon by a substantial number of people as an economic
resource that must be guarded, and in some cases even to the
extent of leaving a job in order to return to the reservation to
qualify for welfare assistance."

During the severe winter of 1947–48, the Turtle Mountain region had been declared a disaster area, and for the first time the
state of North Dakota became seriously concerned about the condition of the Indians. An Indian Affairs Commission was created
at that time, but this commission has largely devoted its efforts
to protecting the North Dakota taxpayers from becoming responsible for the cost of providing services for the Turtle Mountain
Indians.

When the proposal of withdrawing federal support and responsibility was discussed with the Turtle Mountain Indians in
October, 1953, the members expressed amazement that they were
being considered for such action. State and county officials in
North Dakota were equally surprised.

Both the Indians and state officials urged that, before termination should be considered, the federal government undertake a
comprehensive long-range program of economic development,
including land purchase and development, rehousing, and related programs, at an estimated cost of $40,000,000.

Because the Department of the Interior found "little prospect
for alleviation of the social and economic plight of Turtle Mountain people through even the most optimistic assistance and rehabilitation programs," termination legislation was introduced in
January, 1954. The Department adopted the view that it had no
choice in the matter, since the Turtle Mountain Indians had been
cited specifically in Concurrent Resolution 108 as one of the
tribes for which termination legislation was to be submitted to
Congress.

The Department's proposal was a curious effort to reconcile
the necessities of federal withdrawal with the obviously staggering
rehabilitation needs of the people. On the one hand, the formula

contained in the Klamath and other withdrawal bills was proposed here: tribal property would first be personalized; the Indians might create a corporation or other legal entity to manage the property in their behalf, or to liquidate it; and in any case, trusteeship would terminate within five years, if not sooner. On the other hand, recognizing the inadequacy of simply turning these Indians loose, the proposal would require the Secretary to undertake, "within the limits of the funds from time to time appropriated for the purpose," a program of off-reservation resettlement and employment. The Secretary was also authorized to contract for health services for relocated Indians to relieve them of the necessity of returning to the Turtle Mountain Reservation, where the government operates a hospital.

The final element in the compromise formula was a provision that the Secretary would make a determination that relocation had been accomplished "to the extent that it is practicable to accomplish it," and thereupon would publish a proclamation that the trust relationship had been terminated and thereafter the Indians would not be entitled to any of the services performed by the United States for Indians.

If Congress should reduce or even discontinue appropriations for relocation purposes, as it has discontinued money for other programs in the past, it might not be possible for a future Secretary, in good conscience, to declare that relocation had been accomplished for these Indians. Nevertheless, after five years had expired, or sooner, trust restrictions would have been removed from the land, and the complete disintegration of the Turtle Mountain Indians would at last have been accomplished.

Fortunately, the legislation was not adopted.

The same 1953 session of Congress adopted a second major policy declaration that became Public Law 280. This act provided that, with certain exceptions, jurisdiction over criminal offenses and civil causes on reservations in the states of California, Minnesota, Nebraska, Oregon, and Wisconsin would be transferred to state courts; and any other state in which reservations were located might assume the same jurisdiction, on condition that the states enact enabling legislation, without a parallel condition of consent by the affected Indians.

This law provided the means by which one of the last and most important areas of tribal self-government could be wiped out. In 1885, Congress placed the first constraint on the authority of the tribes in the field of law and order by specifying that seven major crimes (later extended to ten) should come within the exclusive jurisdiction of federal courts. With this exception, Congress made no further invasion of the right of the Indian people to acknowledge and live within the customs and social controls of familiar practice.

It is especially noteworthy that President Eisenhower, in consenting to Public Law 280, expressed concern over the failure to provide for consultation with the Indian people and urged that Congress, in its next session, amend the law to correct this oversight. Amendments have since been considered, but none adopted.

The conditions which led to the enactment of this law are worth at least brief notice. A system of Indian police and Indian courts had been instituted in 1878 and operated for years, actually as an administrative convenience of the reservation superintendent. Findings of the Indian courts were not official until they had been approved by the superintendent, in effect making him jury and judge.

The practice was not out of line with the attitudes of the period, which considered the Indians still savage, still needing the firm hand of the white father in Washington. The Indian groups did not object to the white man playing this role, since it did not interfere too seriously with the controls which they exerted through family heads, clan leaders, public opinion within the group, and the devices they knew and respected.

Following the adoption of the Indian Reorganization Act, which recognized the right of the Indian tribe to establish law codes and courts of justice, the Secretary of the Interior in 1935 issued a Code of Indian Offenses which, for the first time, drew a clear line between administrative discretion and the inherent tribal right. This, however, did not meet the problem for those tribes financially unable to pay for the services of police officers and court officials. Appropriations for law-and-order work were made by Congress after that, but never in adequate amounts. As opposition to the general principles of the Indian Reorganization Act gathered force, appropriations for this, as for other tribal purposes, declined further.

With reservation officials no longer at liberty to usurp the field and many tribes unable for financial reasons to administer, law enforcement in many Indian communities failed to function. To some extent assimilation of the Indians had progressed to the point where the old systems no longer could operate; but even in the cases where tribes were prepared to live under state law, lack of funds prevented action.

Some tribes began to request that state enforcement agencies assume responsibility on their reservations. Bills for this purpose were considered in Congress over a period of several years, and early in the opening session of the 83rd Congress such a bill, H.R. 1063, came before the House Committee on Indian Affairs. It proposed to extend state law over the Indian reservations in California. In the course of hearings on this bill, the committee amended it to include the Indians of Minnesota (except the Red Lake Reservation), Oregon (except Warm Springs), Wisconsin (except Menominee), and Nebraska. The Indians of these states were among those who had requested state law. Bills had been introduced in prior Congresses, and hearings had been held. With the exceptions noted, the tribes had agreed to state jurisdiction.

Then, just before the amended legislation went before Congress, two sections were added to it, authorizing all other states to extend their laws over Indian reservations. Tribal consent was not required.

At a conference on Indian tribes and treaties conducted by the University of Minnesota Center for Continuation Study in April, 1955, at which this problem was analyzed and discussed at some length, Henry E. Allen (co-ordinator of student's religious activities, University of Minnesota) offered this observation:

All that we have been hearing points up the fact that we have not yet learned how to establish a policy in America of living with differences. From the time that white people first set foot on the shores of this continent, there has been little genuine appreciation of Indian culture. Instead, we have been uncomfortable because of its manifest differences and have sought by every available means to make the pattern of Indian living conform with what white people regard as a proper arrangement for social and individual life. . . . Particularly, I think we must be sure that the Indian participates fully in the right to determine his own destiny. There must be no arbitrary insistence that the Indian abandon habits, practices, and concepts which give his life meaning and his personality dignity. The Indian must feel that his adaptation to, or his rejection of, the white man's culture are matters for his own determination.[2]

In the area of administrative discretion and action flowing from the policy stated in Concurrent Resolution 108, two incidents deserve attention.

The first of these involves once again the relation of Indians to the land and the intrusion of federal policy into an area which, above all others, will determine Indian survival.

The Indian Reorganization Act did not prohibit the issuance of fee patents to individual Indians holding allotments under trust. Rather, that was accomplished by Order No. 420, issued by the Secretary of the Interior on August 14, 1933, before the passage of the Indian Reorganization Act. This order established the policy that fee patents would not be issued except in cases of emergency, and final determination was left to the Secretary. So carefully was this rule observed that in 1935 only twelve applications for patents-in-fee were approved during the year, covering 1,764 acres.

As the land purchase program developed, effort was made to concentrate purchases within consolidated areas; individual Indians were encouraged to trade their fractions of allotments for tribal lands of equivalent value at one location. A number of tribes supplemented government purchases with their own funds, as part of the general program of consolidating useful economic units of grazing and timber lands.

After World War II, with rising agricultural prices reflected in rising land prices, individual Indian allottees became restive under the restraints of the Bureau land policy. The main recourse of the allottee was to seek relief in Congress. The effect of going to Congress with requests to issue fee patents over the objection of the Secretary of the Interior eventually brought the entire policy under fire and added to the growing dissatisfaction with trusteeship.

The rate at which patents were issued, in spite of these growing pressures, did not at first seriously modify the basic policy. A note of alarm was sounded in the Acting Commissioner's report for 1948, as he observed: "More fee patents were issued during the last fiscal year than in any one year since 1933. The total of 423 patents included 23 which the Secretary of the Interior was directed to issue in private bills adopted by Congress. The area covered by these patents amounted to 67,000 acres. In addition, orders removing restrictions were issued covering an additional 35,000 acres."

The guiding policy was reiterated: "Some isolated Indian holdings can be sold, without endangering the economy of an entire community. Where this possibility exists, fee patents are being issued or restriction against sale is being removed. However, unless the nation is to pauperize the Indian people, discretion must continue to be exercised in issuing patents-in-fee, and that discretion to be effective must be lodged in a responsible official."

The rationalization for Concurrent Resolution 108, couched in terms of emancipating the Indian from bureaucratic controls, was equally a convenient justification for abandoning the effort to conserve and enlarge the Indian land base. The manner in which this occurred is revealed in a Report released by the Senate Committee on Interior and Insular Affairs in December 1958.[3] The Committee Chairman, Senator Murray of Montana, had become so alarmed by the rate at which the Bureau was allowing land to pass out of Indian ownership that he requested a moratorium on further land sales until a study could be made, and the

Secretary of the Interior declared such a moratorium in May, 1958.

The Committee study covered the ten years 1948–1957, and showed that "2,595,413.66 acres of individual trust land were completely removed from all trust status. After subtracting the land acreage in the category of 'takings for public purposes,' the figure emerges as 2,174,517.85 acres removed from individual trust status through actions or approvals of the Bureau of Indian Affairs. . . . After dividing the period under study into two 5-year segments I found that while 804,763.84 acres were removed from 1948 to 1952, inclusive, the period from 1953 to 1957 alone shows 1,790,649.82 acres removed. This shows that my concern at the outset of this study was well founded—individual Indian trust land alienation is climbing at a potentially disastrous rate."

To the Indian people, the most disturbing development in the swiftly changing land policy was an order issued by the Commissioner to his area directors on May 16, 1955. The order authorized these field administrators to issue fee patents, upon the request of the Indian owner, to allotted lands even though the lands be located in areas consolidated for group or community use.

In effect, the order destroyed a basic purpose of the land program. In an economy based on the grazing of livestock, access to water, natural shelter, and other features are of primary importance. The purchase programs of the government and of the tribes were devoted to the acquisition of lands containing such key features or, in case the tribe already possessed key tracts, the effort was directed at acquiring adjacent lands to complete an economic unit. Control of such key tracts meant control of the area; the sale of a key tract almost inevitably forced the sale or lease of the adjoining land, and without water or other desirable features the adjoining landowners had little bargaining power.

The Indian tribes, in protesting to Commissioner Glenn L. Emmons, did not challenge the right of the individual to dispose of his land if he chose. They pleaded, however, for the opportunity to be notified of pending land sales and to meet bids offered by prospective buyers. They also urged, for those tribes that might not have adequate funds, that federal credit be made available to permit tribes to purchase lands from their members, when offered for sale, on long-term repayment contracts.[4]

The Commissioner's order was revised in December, 1955, to provide that, "at the request of the owner," lands might be offered to the tribe or to the individual members or associations of members, by meeting the high bid. No provision for financing land purchases was included.

A former Indian Bureau official, W. O. Roberts, recently retired, sees the consequences of the renewed process of land losses upon the Indians:

Tribal officials in the Dakota country are deeply concerned about the loss of Indian land. They know that when an individual has sold his land and used up his money, he does not stop being an Indian. He simply becomes a landless Indian. The loss of his land adds nothing to his ability or desire to achieve integration into the ways of the white man. . . . The tribal leaders see land, only recently sold to a non-Indian, equipped with a good home, out-buildings, fences, and a fine herd of cattle. And they see the Indian, land and money gone, begging for a handout at the agency office, increasingly dependent on the government for his very existence. . . .

If [the Indians] are abandoned by the government before they can take their place in a community, there is trouble, and it matters little whether the abandonment is by termination of federal services or by the more subtle means of selling out their homesteads. When the Indian land is gone, then the problem will no longer be one of integration, but will become a not very inspiring problem in public relief.[5]

The decision to pursue a firm course of terminating federal responsibility in the Indian field "at the earliest possible time," whether or not Indian agreement is obtained, produces an atmosphere of distrust that may or may not be exaggerated. The fact that it exists at all is indicative of error. It suggests that the methods pursued by the government have not been candid; that full opportunity to negotiate may be denied, and the Indians forced into decisions which they were not prepared to make. They are the methods of the "compulsory process" to "break their habits, and civilize them."

In November, 1954, the year after adoption of Concurrent Resolution 108, the Cherokee Indians of North Carolina were advised that the office of superintendent of their reservation had been abolished. The incumbent, Joe Jennings, would be moved to the Sioux country and his place would not be filled.

The announcement, coming without prior negotiation, not even prior notice, was particularly shattering just then. The Cherokees, working with this superintendent, had accomplished many positive good things and were looking forward to fresh accomplishment.[6]

The Cherokee Indians who live in North Carolina today, known as the Eastern Band of Cherokee Indians, are the descendants of tribal members who succeeded in hiding out when the main body of the tribe was forced, at gun point, to remove west of the Mississippi River. Others returned from exile and joined their kinsmen in the hills, out of sight of the government. They began to acquire land, some of it by gift and some by individual purchases. These purchases were made in the name of a trader friend, William H. Thomas, in order not to divulge their identity. They were by no means sure that the federal government would allow them to remain if their presence became known. Their faith in this one white man was not betrayed, as it had been betrayed by other white men. He kept the land in his name, kept the taxes paid. Finally the group incorporated under North Carolina state law, and title to the land was transferred to this corporation.

An act of Congress of 1876 gave official recognition to the Qualla Reservation, thus establishing the right of the Eastern Cherokees to retain their new home. Not until 1924 were they sufficiently reconciled to the intentions of government as to request legislation bringing their Qualla Reservation, and lands added later, under the trusteeship of the United States.

The land was poor, rocky, much of it rising in sheer hillsides from the creeks and streams that abounded. But also there were narrow valleys twisting into the hills, and in these the Cherokees planted their fields as they had done before the white man came. The government accepted trusteeship of the land in 1924, and built schools and a little hospital.

When Jennings became superintendent in 1945, the people were in poor condition. The little farms in the valleys and on the hillsides were never quite large enough to support a family; through years of cropping, the land had exhausted its fertility and was eroding away. Wage employment was hard to find and the Cherokees were hungry.

Jennings bent his first efforts on helping the people to rebuild the soil and to see the necessity of this. With them he soon developed a strong soil conservation program—cover crops were plowed under, and in return the government donated fertilizer. They began to plow their hills on the contour. Jennings started community improvement programs. As a first project, he helped one community to install painted mailboxes along a rural route. Barns and houses were painted, using a composition of red brick dust and used crankcase oil that cost almost nothing but the labor of application. Eventually six community improvement associations were organized, and in competition with eighty other communities, all white, located in western North Carolina, one of the Cherokee communities won second prize. The effect on Cherokee morale was electrifying.

The communities and civic organizations of the area were interested in the Cherokee people and would help when called upon. Jennings found, upon his arrival, that the Cherokees were being denied the right of franchise, even though citizens, largely because of the personal opposition of a few local officials. When Jennings presented the situation to the local post of the American Legion, in which some Cherokees held membership, response was immediate. With the help of the Legion the rights of the Cherokees were soon restored.

The reservation is situated just at the southern entrance to the Great Smoky Mountains National Park. The Cherokees decided to take advantage of their situation to benefit from the tourist trade. With some small funds of their own and additional funds borrowed from the Bureau's revolving credit fund, they built a handsome stone tourist lodge and restaurant, later adding a service station. The National Park Service helped them with the design and landscaping, and the result was a group of buildings that the entire region points to with pride.

By all odds, the crowning achievement of the renascent Cherokees was the planning, organization, and ultimate production of the historical pageant called *Unto These Hills*. It is the story of "the trail of tears," the forced removal of the people in the awful winter of 1838–39.

In creating the pageant the Cherokees worked with Paul Green of the dramatics department of the University of North Carolina and Kermit Hunter, who did the actual writing. The Cherokee Historical Association was formed to serve as sponsor and producer, the association being made up of local professional and business people, Indian and white. A natural amphitheater was developed for the production, and the seating capacity of 2,900 is filled every summer night from June until September. In its first five years more than 750,000 spectators witnessed the pageant, which has a cast of 140 actors, most of them amateurs, most of them drawn from the Cherokee tribe.

In that five-year period the Cherokee Historical Association, as producer, paid out $389,831 in salaries to Cherokee employees and actors; purchased $27,000 worth of supplies from members of the tribe; contributed $29,000 to the tribal treasury for community services, $76,000 for educational benefits, $18,777 for community development, and about $50,000 in construction.

With $60,000 donated by the State of North Carolina and funds supplied by the Cherokee Historical Association, an authentic Indian village was constructed adjacent to the outdoor theater. In its own way, the reconstruction is as valid as Williamsburg of Virginia; without lavish expenditure, it portrays the Cherokee people in the dress and common occupations of an earlier day.

Encouraged by the tribal example, a number of individual Cherokees have since built tourist accommodations, including stores and filling stations, and are earning separate incomes.

Craft workers have been encouraged and indeed have been

quite successful in marketing their products. The workers organized an arts and crafts board and a co-operative sales organization which realizes sales of more than $100,000 a year.

The Cherokee Tribal Fair has become a major attraction in the region. Organized in 1917 and operated entirely by members of the tribe, it features exhibits of arts and crafts, farm products, 4-H Club work, and the spirited Indian ball game, in which spectators delight.

The Cherokees responded in many ways, once the doors were open. They participated in community organizations such as the Kiwanis Club, American Legion, Association of American University Women, Western North Carolina Historical Association, Southern Highlands Handicraft Guild, and Boy Scouts and Girl Scouts. Their own community associations and their tribal council grew in effectiveness and in their contacts with the surrounding area. The state universities of Tennessee, Georgia, and North Carolina established at Cherokee, agency headquarters, a permanent historical museum, and Tsali Institute. Faculty members of the University of North Carolina helped in the development of a plan for the town of Cherokee, also an area plan for the reservation. The tribe became a member of the regional planning association for western North Carolina.

In the winter of 1953–54, Haverford College in Pennsylvania used the Cherokee Reservation as a field laboratory in which to conduct a seminar workshop for a graduate unit of its social and technical assistance program.

All of this was in the background when Superintendent Jennings was notified on November 12, 1954, that his position had been abolished. The Indians could not believe it, neither could the neighoring communities and citizens. One of the leading newspapers of the area, the *Asheville Citizen*, denounced the action as "summary," and as destructive of the orderly process of transition from wardship to full participation in American life of the Cherokee people. Civic leaders in three states, newspapers, university professors, and the congressional delegation from North Carolina promptly protested.

Then the people of the area saw that there had been purpose

operating for some time, but they had not realized it. The administration of law and order, some time before, had been transferred to the state. There had been no objection to that, since it moved in the direction in which the Indians seemed to be going. When the boarding school was closed, that too seemed to be part of an orderly procedure. When it was proposed that the hospital be transferred to an operating organization other than the government, the local agency and the tribal council working together started negotiations with several groups, including one church group that had a long and favorable record for successful hospital administration. This matter was taken out of their hands and the transfer was made to the United States Public Health Service instead.

The beef and dairy herds formerly attached to the boarding school were sold off. The noon meal, which the day schools served the children, giving employment to a few Cherokee women, was, without prior explanation, given as a concession to a food caterer in Washington, D.C.

Public dismay and protests brought belated explanations; but these did not undo the damage.

According to the explanations, the decisions at Cherokee were not in the nature of major policy reversals, only administrative changes. Superintendent Jennings was not, as first ordered, required to report to an inconsequential position in South Dakota but was to be brought into Washington in a consultative capacity. The position had not been abolished, and a new superintendent would be appointed. The cattle had been sold because the boarding school had been closed. The child-feeding contract was an experiment to determine whether the centralization of food services saved money. When the new superintendent arrived after Jennings' departure, he read a statement from Commissioner Emmons, which read in part: "Somehow or other the impression has been created that we are going to abolish the agency, liquidate all our functions and programs and simply walk out on the job without so much as a by your leave. Nothing could be further from the truth."

The spirit in which Concurrent Resolution 108 is written

springs from an impatience that is neither warranted nor calculated to inspire confidence. The phrasing "as rapidly as possible" and "at the earliest possible time" is not an assurance of justice expedited, but rather of one-sided decisions rushed to consummation.

At Cherokee, the nettle of impatience was not warranted. The people were moving, as their ancestors had moved more than a century before. In that earlier period, after the people had been torn up by the roots and marched a thousand miles away, they sat down and planned a new life. So this smaller Eastern Band, after the Bureau had rushed in and then rushed out again, sat down to plan its future.

The tribal council, meeting in March, 1955, adopted its own program for the gradual transfer of facilities and responsibilities. The items approved by the tribal council were these: (1) Ask Congress to authorize revision of the tribal roll, which had not been brought up to date in thirty-one years. (2) Make a land survey and register the Indians' possessory rights. (3) Maintain an adequate health program, including hospital facilities for all members of the tribe. (4) Upgrade and properly house the schools and turn them over to North Carolina. (5) Set up a plan to bring industrial enterprises to the reservation. (6) Improve housing standards, since most Indians lived in one- or two-room houses. (7) Conserve forests, soil, game, and fish.

The administration of Indian affairs, once more, was challenged by Indian patience and Indian charity.

XVIII

THE LONG VIEW

THE divergent views that alternately have blessed and menaced the record of Government-Indian relations can be reconciled. The ultimate achievement of sound government policy in this field requires that they be reconciled.

In the Navajo record, as that record stands today, they have been reconciled. Navajo tribal self-government is respected and encouraged. Navajo tribal property rights are protected and tribal holdings have been steadily expanded. The strenuous efforts made in recent years to provide schools for Navajo children indicate a desire to bring the Navajo people into fuller participation in the American community. That desire must reflect a conclusion that the Navajos are a worthy people, capable of profiting from the white man's schools.[1]

How did it happen that the Navajo tribe, the one-time incorrigible raiders of the Southwest, managed to avoid the consequences of the "compulsory process" and win the right to hold fast to their institutions? The question could be asked also of the Rio Grande Pueblos and of the Zuni and Hopi in the west. Something in these people never yielded.

All of them, in the course of their contacts with the incoming white man, experienced varying degrees of violence. The Navajos endured the humiliation of being rounded up like wild cattle and marched off to an exile that lasted for four years. But they came back from that, and prospered. What quality was it that brought them through privation and outrage and kept them from breaking?

The answer is not in tight social organization, such as characterizes the Pueblo city-states, for Navajo society was never closely knit. Neither was it in any pervasive, unifying ideal, as Christianity was in European society. The question is raised here, not answered.

From what is known and what can be surmised of their history, the Navajos have been an adaptable people. Coming down out of the plains of Canada (their linguistic kinsmen, the Athabascan tribes, are found today scattered all the way to the Arctic Circle), they reached the southwestern United States some time after A.D. 1000. They and the people now called Apaches were probably indistinguishable when they came out of the north, the Navajos remaining a core people, while the Apaches split into a number of distinct bands. The once common language broke first into two fragments, Navajo and Apache, and the latter tended to develop further dialectic differences. The division into two groups probably had not been completed when the Spaniards entered northern New Mexico in the middle of the sixteenth century. At least, the Navajos were first identified by the name *Apaches de Nabahu,* a Pueblo term translated as "people of the big planted fields."

While the Navajos caused grief to the settled Pueblo peoples by raiding their fields, they also became good neighbors. After the Pueblo rebellion of 1680, when the Rio Grande tribes, fearing Spanish reprisals, fled westward, they found the Navajos good hosts and strong allies. For the Navajos, it was a time of learning and change. Their language felt the influence, and the event may account for the initial differentiation from Apache. They began to plant their own fields, either then or just before. They acquired sheep. Soon they were weaving wool. Still later, they would learn to work in silver and to set turquoise stones in their jewelry. Probably the greatest flowering of those early years was in the ceremonial practices which so characterize their lives today.

They came out of the north as hunters, with the simplest equipment and organization. They developed into accomplished agri-

culturists and herdsmen, and in the same process of years created
a mythology and ritualism of amazing beauty and vigor.

So thoroughly dependent had the Navajos become on their
fields and flocks by the nineteenth century that when repeated
efforts of the United States Army failed to subdue their boister-
ous raiding, Kit Carson managed very well against them by killing off their sheep and goats, destroying their cornfields, and
chopping down their peach trees. Soon the people were starving
and readily surrendered in return for Army rations issued at
Fort Defiance. When they had all been rounded up in 1864, they
were marched off to Fort Sumner in eastern New Mexico, three
hundred miles away.

This was the "big walk" which broke their spirits and ended
their days of raiding. They remained in captivity for four years,
and so defeated were they that when General Sherman came out
to report on their condition in 1868, they fell to the ground before
him and begged to be released.

In the treaty they signed, the Navajos promised to keep to
peaceful ways, a promise they never broke. The United States
made promises as well: sheep to replace those slaughtered, seed
to plant and implements to till the soil, rations, and schools.

The issuance of rations led to the demoralization of a number
of tribes—but not the Navajo tribe. As soon as the people were
released with their pairs of sheep or goats and their bags of corn,
they scattered over the land, back to the canyons and sheltered
valleys they had known. Soon they were feeding themselves
again.

In the next sixty years they made a recovery that was truly
remarkable. The population increased more than fourfold, from
the 9,000 enumerated in captivity to more than 40,000 by 1930.
(At present, the population is estimated at 80,000.)

The increase of livestock was equally startling, considering
that they were no longer at liberty to appropriate the herds of
their neighbors. The gains they made had to be honestly earned.

Upon their return from Fort Sumner, the government issued
a total of 35,000 sheep and goats over a period of several years.
By 1930, these figures had increased to 574,821 sheep, 186,768

goats, 25,000 head of cattle, and 50,000 head of horses. Counting each horse as the equivalent of five sheep and each cow as the equivalent of four, in the amount of forage consumed, this was the equivalent of 1,111,589 sheep units.[2]

During those first years no thought was given to achieving a balance between land and livestock. This was generally true in the western grazing country, where every operator strove to acquire more land and larger herds. The Navajos prospered in those years. The reservation created for them by the Treaty of 1868, consisting of 3,500,000 acres, did not contain the Navajo people and they returned to occupy many of the areas they had used before the Fort Sumner exile. By a series of executive-order extensions and congressional acts, lands were annexed to the treaty reservation, until by 1938 the reservation consisted of approximately 15,500,000 acres and more than half a million acres had been transferred to them as individual allotments on the public domain in New Mexico.

Even with the enlargement of the land base, the growing disparity between resources and population became apparent. At first, herds concentrated around the relatively few watering places and the surrounding range was depleted. In 1893, the problem became so serious that Congress appropriated the first funds for water development. There was no systematic effort made to control grazing, and no accurate livestock counts were made until the problem was attacked jointly by the Indian Bureau and the Department of Agriculture in 1933.

By that time destruction of the range through overgrazing was approaching disaster. Technicians who studied conditions in minute detail found that the maximum carrying capacity of the land was 560,000 sheep units. The land had been carrying double that load for an undetermined number of years. Drought conditions growing steadily more severe intensified the destruction. Fresh-water lakes, which once were abundant in some areas, disappeared, their beds filled with siltation and their waters evaporated. Perennial streams expired. Ground water receded until springs and artesian wells no longer functioned.

A 1935 study by range experts reached this disturbing conclusion: "Within the reservation there has been brought about a progressively deterioraing situation which, if allowed to continue, would ultimately make the area virtually uninhabitable and will force the United States to remove the Indian population, and resettle them or support them on a dole, a procedure which in turn would destroy the resources of much of the non-Indian population surrounding the reservation, which is dependent on trade with the Indians and on tourist activities."

The technical men could see the situation clearly: it meant reduction of the livestock load by more than half, and, to be effective, the reduction should take place promptly.

To the Navajo Indians, when this information was interpreted to them, the conclusion had a shattering effect. Livestock meant food, but it meant more than that. Herds were a measure of prestige. The herds might be overage and not fully productive, but a man's worth was judged by the size of the herds. Horses, which had no economic value to the family, except as transportation, were a particular mark of distinction.

The livestock reduction program created bitterness and a sense of humiliation as intense, perhaps, as the imprisonment at Fort Sumner. The Navajos were sent to Fort Sumner because they had challenged the power of the white man; but the sheep reduction, which took food out of their mouths, was inflicted on them for doing the very things they had been encouraged to do.

Nevertheless, the alternatives were clear, and the technical men went forward, invoking the legal authority of the Secretary of the Interior on occasion, bringing tribal government almost to destruction in the process, but finally the objective was achieved. In 1941, on the eve of World War II, the livestock load was down to the carrying capacity of the range.

The economic effect of the reduction program, in terms of income, actually made for improvement. The animals taken off the range were the cull animals that had no market value, and emphasis was placed on retaining young breeding ewes. Excess horses were removed and families were encouraged to keep only young stuff, limited to the number they actually needed for transportation and for herding. A sheep-breeding laboratory, es-

tablished at the very start of the reduction program, resulted in
introducing improved breeding strains throughout the Navajo
country.

The effects of improved breeding practices began to be felt almost immediately. The younger breeding stock produced a
higher percentage of lambs, the lambs tended to be heavier, and
the production of wool increased remarkably. In 1935, for example, 550,000 head of sheep produced just over 2,000,000
pounds of wool; in 1941, when the livestock load had been
brought down to estimated carrying capacity, 434,000 head of
sheep produced more than 3,000,000 pounds of wool. Income
from livestock actually increased through the years in which reduction took effect.

During those years also, income was greatly increased as a
result of the funds spent on the reservation in soil and moisture
conservation work, the building of roads and truck trails, forest
management, the building of irrigation works and the development of underground water, and the construction of schools and
other facilities.

The war years brought entirely new conditions. Livestock and
agricultural prices increased steadily, and the income of those
who stayed on the land benefited accordingly. Employment on
the reservation disappeared as peacetime civilian programs came
to an end. This was more than made up for by employment opportunities away from the reservation. As many as 15,000 Navajos
took advantage of off-reservation employment, some of them going into seasonal agricultural work, but many went into war
industries as far away as the Middle West and the Pacific coast.

In the first stages of the war, young Navajos were rejected for
military duty if they were non-English-speaking. Later, as man-
power needs grew acute and special training courses were developed, Navajos were accepted and trained, and eventually
3,600 saw duty in the armed services. They made an outstanding
record in the Marine Corps as "code talkers," in which they used
the Navajo language to relay information from advanced posts
with assault waves to supporting positions in the rear.

Income from wartime employment and from servicemen's allotment checks resulted in an estimated family income of $1,200 per year. The average annual family income in 1940 had been estimated at $410.

The situation of the Navajo people deterioriated rapidly after the war. The prewar reservation programs were not immediately renewed. War workers and servicemen returned from distant places, and suddenly people were hungry and idle.

The Navajos themselves took the lead in making their conditions known and asking for assistance. In the spring of 1946 a delegation of twenty-six, consisting of the chairman and vice-chairman and outstanding leaders in the tribal council, traveled to Washington to appear before officials in the Department of Interior, the Budget Bureau, and the Appropriations Committees in House and Senate.

Chee Dodge, the chairman, appearing before the Senate Committee on Indian Affairs, made plain his purpose: "We are here for the purpose of seeking aid on behalf of our people. We are handicapped to a great extent on the reservation with regard to our educational setup. Our forefathers made a treaty with the government of the United States in 1868 and we are here seeking the fulfillment of that treaty agreement."

Scott Preston, leader from Tuba City, Arizona, explained what had been happening in Navajo thinking:

First of all, we found ourselves in a handicapped position when war was declared by the United States. If we were called to serve with other people, we were handicapped because we were unable to understand anything outside of the Navajo language. With that handicap we cannot help ourselves on the reservation. We had difficulty in that respect with selective service. We were not trained in any given work. We were not able to do anything to help along as much as we would have liked.

We found ourselves in a handicapped position there right away. We started thinking that there was something lacking that we should have and we said it was education. If we were educated we would be doing the things the other people were doing to win this war. That just started us to think about it. . . .

Not only were we handicapped from the standpoint of education in language and trade but on the other hand there is a pressure put upon the whole reservation to save it from deterioration by the elimination of what had been our personal support—livestock. It has dwindled down to much less than we had and we cannot rely on that for a living in the future. We have to look elsewhere.[3]

The delegates talked about being trained for trades, and a committee member asked if a Navajo, after learning a trade, would be willing to leave the reservation in order to follow the trade.

Scott Preston was prompt in answering: "That is exactly what we mean. If a man from New Mexico or Arizona learns a trade and can do better in New York City he should be able to go there or any other place."

It was clear from the testimony of the delegates that Navajo attitudes toward schools and toward the white man and his world had changed. But what was not clear then, and would not become clear until several years had passed, was the permanency of the change. Were the Navajos, in their desperate need for help of every kind, concentrating their appeal on schools and hospitals because they knew the white men in Congress would be most inclined to respond to such an appeal? Did they really have the support of the great body of the tribe, 80 to 90 per cent of which was non-English-speaking and kept itself carefully isolated from the outside?

It was true that the Treaty of 1868 had promised schools for the Navajo people, but the promise had placed obligations on the Navajo people as well as on the government. In Article VI of the Treaty, the Navajo signatories pledged "themselves to compel their children, male and female, between the ages of six and sixteen years, to attend school. . . ." The United States, for its part, agreed that "for every thirty children between said ages who can be induced or compelled to attend school, a schoolhouse shall be provided, and a teacher competent to teach the elementary branches of an English education shall be furnished. . . ."

From the treaty period down to recent times, the white man's

school occupied at best a peripheral place in Navajo life. The
things the schools could teach were not essential to Navajo practices, and in many ways were inimical to Navajo values. A child
became part of the adult world at an early age. The learning
process started early, and the child that was to survive into adulthood could not afford to stop learning. His crops had to grow in
the absence of sufficient water. His sheep had to be taken where
there was forage, but without overtiring them, and where they
would find water. They had to be protected from predators. The
growing child must learn how to be respectful, how to behave,
how to protect himself against the evil things that caused illness. It
was not a matter of the economic worth of the child to the family,
as some writers have mentioned; it had rather to do with the child
growing in a natural way into responsible adulthood. In any
society, this is the purpose of education. The Navajos understood
and trusted their own ways; they neither understood nor trusted
the white man's system.

The nature of the change reflected in the testimony of the
tribal delegates is illustrated in two incidents, described by Allan
G. Harper, formerly area director for the Bureau of Indian Affairs
at Window Rock, Arizona, headquarters for the Navajo reservation. The first incident involved David L. Shipley, superintendent
of the Navajo Agency at Fort Defiance, Arizona, in 1890 and for
some years thereafter:

By 1892, Mr. Shipley had developed a more vigorous technique of
recruiting which in turn developed more vigorous resistance. One day
while recruiting students at Round Rock, Mr. Shipley found himself
confronted by a warlike band, led by a head man named Black Horse,
all violently opposed to turning over Navajo children to the white man
for training and education.

In the clash that ensued, Shipley was injured, then rescued by the
intervention of a few Navajos and carried to the trading post where he
and a few companions barricaded themselves until the arrival of troops
made their safe return to Fort Defiance possible.

The leaky and altogether wretched school in the Fort for which
Mr. Shipley sought students was otherwise circumvented: reports of
that period state that pupils, having been enticed to register, and hav-

ing been issued new clothing, were apt to slip off into the night never to return. . . .

In August of 1949, the contrasting incident occurred when hundreds of children—over and above those already selected for attendance at off-reservation boarding schools—presented themselves at collecting points on the reservation in the vain hope that they, too, could get some education.

Our school personnel explained the woeful limitations of school space and reluctantly told the overflow of children to go home. Yet later at the two principal dispatch centers (Tuba City and Fort Wingate) there appeared scores of eager, unsolicited children who again had to be rejected, and turned homeward.[4]

The nature and significance of the change were studied by John Adair, who interviewed a number of Navajo and Pueblo war veterans after their return to their home communities. He too was impressed by the factors that came under his observation.

There was a long continuum of change on these reservations caused by events going back some years before our entry into the conflict: the initiation of the Selective Service Act, the rationing of food, the building of war industries, such as the munitions depot at Fort Wingate, New Mexico, and Bellemont, Arizona, and later the Division of the Manhattan Project at Los Alamos. The superintendents of the different reservations had seen not only the steady flow of young men leaving for duty in the armed service, but they saw whole families pick up their most essential possessions and leave the reservations for war work. . . . They saw the allotment checks come home to dependents, the boys returning on furlough, and the tremendous wages paid by the war industries—experiences common to the country at large, but brought into sharper focus on the Indian reservations in the southwest where such prosperity was heretofore unknown. . . . The cash income of the Navajo tribe more than doubled; great quantities of store goods were purchased and most of the weavers laid aside their wool cards and spindles until after the war work and allotment checks dried up. . . .

It is my conclusion after having interviewed over a hundred veterans during this past summer, and observing many more at various ceremonials and other large gatherings, that the period of this second World War has exerted a great impact on the cultures of these peoples, perhaps the greatest since the arrival of the Spaniards 400 years ago. . . .[5]

The summer of 1947 was a season of severe drought. In spite of the drastic livestock reduction, the range had not recovered, and now the people faced disaster. The plight of the Navajos was brought to the attention of the nation partly by chance, though their needs were so real as to merit public notice. During that summer Secretary of State Marshall had invited the European nations to participate, with the help of the United States, in a European Recovery Program (Marshall Plan). Political opponents of the administration, searching for arguments against the sending of American aid to foreign countries, picked up the case of the needy Navajos and used it as a club. Why send money abroad when our own people are starving? was the argument.

The Navajo situation became so well publicized by newspapers seeking to embarrass the administration that three separate congressional subcommittees visited the reservation during the latter part of 1947. A report of the House Public Lands Committee issued on November 24, 1947, recommended an emergency appropriation of $2,000,000. On December 2, 1947, President Truman released a statement expressing his concern and urged the Congress to act on a long-range rehabilitation measure, which the Secretary of the Interior had just submitted to him.[6]

On December 12, 1947, Congress authorized an appropriation of $2,000,000 for the immediate relief of the Navajo and Hopi Indians, and directed the Secretary of the Interior "at the earliest practical date to submit to the Congress his recommendation for necessary legislation for a long range program dealing with the problems of the Navajo and Hopi Indians."

Further spur to action came, again fortuitously, in the winter of 1948–49. A blizzard which struck at the end of January closed roads and piled snow so deep that sheep were unable to graze. Rarely do Navajo families have food for themselves or feed for their livestock in reserve against emergency needs. In a matter of days the stormbound families were faced with starvation, along with their flocks. In this desperate situation, the Navajo Agency and tribe, the Army, National Guard, and Civil Air Patrol, on the ground and in the air, organized a rescue mission. Bags of food and bales of hay were flown over the stricken areas and dropped within reach of the scattered hogans. No lives were lost through starvation, but about 10 per cent of the livestock either starved or froze to death.

What emerged finally from this long ordeal of frustration and acute privation was a long-range rehabilitation program for the Navajo and Hopi Indians—the Hopi reservation being completely encircled by Navajo lands and sharing the same climatic and economic hazards. The program was approved by the act of Congress of April 1, 1950, authorizing an expenditure of $88,570,000 over a ten-year period.[7]

The purposes for which the money could be used are of great interest, since they were designed to provide a co-ordinated attack on the problems of poverty, illiteracy, lack of communications, poor health, and isolation from American society which accounted for the Navajo plight. The headings included soil and water conservation and range improvement; the completing or extension of irrigation projects, including feasibility studies of an irrigation dam on the San Juan River; surveys of timber, coal, mineral, and other physical and human resources; development of industrial and business enterprises; assistance in obtaining off-reservation employment; resettlement of Navajo and Hopi Indians on irrigated lands of the Colorado River Indian Reservation; roads and trails; telephone and radio communication systems; agency, institutional, and domestic water supply; establishment of a revolving-loan fund; hospital buildings and equipment; school buildings and equipment; housing and necessary facilities.

Of equal interest is the statement of purposes contained in the act and the methods to be followed in its administration.

The purpose was "To make available the resources of their [Navajo and Hopi] reservations for use in promoting a self-supporting economy and self-reliant communities, and to lay a stable foundation on which these Indians can engage in diversified economic activities and ultimately attain standards of living, comparable with those enjoyed by other citizens. . . ."

Other sections of the act authorized the Navajo tribe to adopt a constitution (the Hopi Indians had, under the Indian Reorganization Act); required the Bureau of Indian Affairs to consult with the Navajos and Hopis in the development of the program, and to report each year to Congress; gave preference to Navajos and Hopis in construction work, and specified that job training be included in all construction projects.

At the time this program was presented to Congress in 1948, Acting Commissioner William Zimmerman, Jr., observed:

Apart from the meaning which the proposed investment in resource development must have to a people as poorly situated as are the Navajo and Hopi Indians, the presentation of this program is important because it is the first time that a plan for a specific Indian area has reached the stage of Congressional consideration. Other such plans are in the making; indeed, they have been taking shape over a period of years. Acceptance or rejection of the Navajo-Hopi proposal may determine whether our national Indian policy in the future is to be based on a division of the total problem of human adjustment and resource utilization into parcels of a size that can be measured and dealt with on a time schedule.

And he pointed out, in his report for that year, that the Navajo-Hopi program represented the kind of approach to Indian affairs administration that had been recommended in the Meriam survey twenty years before. As was stated on that occasion: "The most fundamental step that can be taken is to advance the economic and social conditions of the Indians of each jurisdiction, with due regard to the economic resources of that jurisdiction, and to supply each jurisdiction with a sufficient number of properly trained workers to make that program effective."

The "other such plans" mentioned by the Acting Commissioner never got through Congress, though several were introduced as bills and hearings were held. Possibly the other tribes did not get enough newspaper publicity; perhaps they were not near enough to starvation—though they might dispute this.

The Navajo-Hopi program, modified in some of its details and time schedules, remains as the guide to administration for those reservations. The monies authorized under the long-range program, of course, are only part of the total funds appropriated each year. The long-range-program money is over and above regular operating budget items. It provides the means for the capital construction and resource development which other reservations never receive.

A further result of the long-range program and the requirement of co-operative planning with the Indian people is that the Navajo tribe, through its elected leaders, has learned the value and something of the methods of social and economic planning. Within the last few years, as the tribe has acquired income from oil and gas leasing and the exploitation of uranium and other minerals, its governing body has exercised caution, yet a growing skill, in the management of finances.

The trait of adaptability still operates in the lives of these people. The tribal council, which government administrators created thirty years ago as a legal device to validate mineral leases on tribal lands, has today become a responsible governing body, giving effective voice to the needs and aspirations of 80,000 people. Until the advent of this representative council, the Navajos had never known centralized government.

Adaptation takes place at the local level as well. At Crownpoint, New Mexico, administrative center for the eastern Navajo country, the leaders from a number of outlying communities have been meeting at regular intervals over a five-year period. This in itself is a departure from the past, in which leadership was exercised by headmen within a circumscribed geographical area and only on rare occasions would two or more leaders join forces. The Crownpoint district includes some seventeen local communities, or chapters, and an estimated 20,000 Navajos. Since they had no meeting place, the leaders first decided to construct a community meeting house, and volunteered their labor for the purpose. Later they remodeled an abandoned government building to provide a community laundry. A place for women to sew, social activities for the young, a place to read and to listen to radio broadcasts, a weekly motion picture program, classes conducted by the county extension and home demonstration agents, shower baths for the family, a bed for the night—all these were soon incorporated in a community program made possible by leaders accepting responsibility.

The discussions carried on in the Crownpoint community house provided information and learning opportunities for the entire area. Also the discussions resulted in specific proposals for the administration of tribal land, for expanded school facilities, for better roads, for domestic water development, and for improved law enforcement and social services.

These activities were encouraged by American Indian Development, a privately financed project in citizenship education. The project defined its purpose as one of helping the people to identify problems and, with them, of finding sources of technical and material help, such as was needed in constructing the community building.

The response to this outside, nonofficial help demonstrated not only that the Navajos are still an adaptable people, but that, when possessed of information needed for action, their judgments are instinctively sound. Although the great majority are non-English-speaking, their grasp on reality is efficient.

This suggests that if their ability to plan and to manage their affairs is not destroyed by legislation or administrative regulation, the Navajo people will make the adaptations that are needed to secure their future. But the Navajos are not unique among the Indian people. The quality of judgment and the perception of reality are of the same order among all Indian groups.

At the moment, the difference is that, at Navajo, the "compulsory" process has yielded to a democratic process. The people are encouraged to develop self-government and to use native custom and practice. This seems to fit better in the American tradition of respecting the individual.

XIX

UNFINISHED TASK

It is a commonplace to hear it said that the United States has administered Indian affairs for more than one hundred years and should get out of the business.

Interpreted in action proposals, getting out of the business means liquidating the Indian reservations, as Menominee and Klamath are being liquidated.

It means turning Indians loose by personalizing the property of the tribes and giving the individual members a vested title.

It means making "first-class citizens" of the Indians by first impoverishing them, then disclaiming any further responsibility for them.

The list of perverted beneficences could be extended, to no advantage. They all arise out of ignorance of the fact, or distortion of the fact, or possibly motives more malign than ignorance or mere willfulness.

Looking back over the record that has been sketched in these pages, it is obvious that there has been no administration of Indian affairs deserving of that description until within the last thirty years. Administration implies management, and management surely presupposes a beneficial purpose. The legislative and executive branches of government acted in the field of Indian affairs, and consequences flowed from the actions. Indians lost land and other things of value; their freedoms were curtailed by reason of those actions. To say that their affairs were administered is to abuse the term.

The Indian Removal Act of 1830 and the Trade and Intercourse

Act of 1834, as examples of early statutory treatment of the subject, were concerned with extending and defining the authority of
the executive. Subsequent legislation followed the same pattern.
The first general policy pronouncement was the decision in 1871
to discontinue the practice of treaty negotiation with Indian tribes.
That was an injunction aimed at Congress and it offered no
guidance to administration.

The General Allotment Act of 1887 was a declaration of policy
and it set the bounds in which Indian affairs were conducted for
the next forty-five years. In that period there was no management
for a beneficial purpose; there was, instead, dismemberment and
dissipation of the Indian estate.

Not until publication of the Meriam survey report were the
basic requirements of an administration of Indian affairs made
available. These requirements are (1) facts about the situation
with which administration is to deal, (2) objectives of administration, and (3) the policy that is to determine how those objectives
are attained.

The Meriam report was not an adequate guide to action in
many respects. The fact that it is repeatedly referred to in previous pages is an indication of how greatly the survey was needed
and how close it came to supplying an objective study of Indian
conditions; but this is not to overlook its defects. It was hastily
conducted. The ten-member team had seven months in which to
visit and observe more than one hundred Indian agencies, separate schools and hospitals, and other field stations. Only one
agency seems to have been visited by all ten members; twenty-
two agencies were visited by a single staff member. This division
of labor and travel time reduced opportunities for staff members
to exchange information and observations.

A more serious criticism of the staff findings (and it might be
directed at the composition of the staff) was the failure to investigate and report on Indian society itself. How much of it still
functioned, in what forms, with what expectations and aspirations, and in what respects at variance with the dominant society?
In the absence of this kind of information, the recommendations
are in many respects the very recommendations that such a study

group might propose for a typical rural white community lacking resources, credit, and basic social services.

These shortcomings did not detract seriously from the value of the report, which remains today the first serious effort to arrive at a comprehensive statement of conditions and to propose remedies.

Administration of Indian affairs, if any regard is to be had for the meaning of the words, starts with 1928.

The accomplishments of at least the first two decades of this thirty-year span were not inconsiderable. Viewed against the previous record of wastage of assets and demoralization of the Indian people, the period 1928–48 was one in which the government faced up to its responsibilities and the Indian people took fresh hope.

If the Indians responded in no other way, their success in forming the National Congress of American Indians in 1944, and maintaining it as an active advocate of their interests, would be a measure of their growth. Earlier attempts at forming a national Indian organization had failed. The people had no sense of a common cause; their experiences in organization methods had been negligible; they had only vague notions about the ways of government and the mechanics of legislation, as these are practiced by white men. This was soon remedied by the practical experiences the tribes derived from the governments they established under the Indian Reorganization Act. Parliamentary procedures did not sit comfortably with them at first. Rule of the majority, for most tribes, was alien and hard to accept. But election to tribal office moved some individuals to present themselves as candidates for county and state offices. A few even looked ahead to winning a seat in Congress.

The forming of the National Congress was a logical development in the growing political consciousness of the Indian people.

What of the future? What remains to be done and how will this best be accomplished?

But first, what is the nature of the problem? To dismiss this question, to decide that it is of no consequence, is to conclude that the mistakes of the past must be repeated. It is to conclude that because the Indians are a small people they are not able to judge matters for themselves, and the privilege of judgment must be assumed in their behalf by an authority which must be correct because it is more powerful.

This point of view is well stated in a report issued in September, 1954, by the House Subcommittee on Indian Affairs. The subcommittee is distressed to find that "Apparently no law yet enacted in the field of Indian affairs has had the effect of stimulating Indians, as a group, to make an active effort to end federal wardship."[1]

The implication behind this is that if the right law can be conceived and adopted by Congress, the problem of the Indians will dissolve into mist. It was to achieve just such an easy solution that termination laws were adopted for the Klamath and other tribes in that same 83rd Congress.

Disregarding the ambiguous and misleading term "wardship" and assuming, with the writer of the subcommittee report, that the term refers to an undesirable situation and Indians could best help themselves by abandoning that status, this presumably would involve changes of attitude and practice in the Indian people. But change of the nature involved cannot be achieved by legislation. The failure of the Allotment Act should persuade us of that.

Change is something that occurs inside of people. It occurs, evidently, when something happens that causes people either to be dissatisfied with something they have, in which case they will try to be rid of it, or to find something desirable to add to what they already have, in which case they will adopt it. But decisions of this nature are not made under duress; if made at all, they are made in a climate offering freedom of choice, in which the inducements are seen as individual growth.

Professor Sol Tax, chairman of the Department of Anthropology at the University of Chicago, has observed and worked closely with the little community of Sac and Fox Indians at Tama, Iowa. This Indian community, completely surrounded by corn-belt farm society since 1857, has remained basically Indian.

Professor Tax explores their motives:

What about Indian resistance to change? It seems to us that most of these Indians will not make a change which (1) requires them to switch their identification; if a change requires that they desert their group and their group symbols. Probably only Indians already expatriated will change. (2) Nor will most of these Indians make changes that would violate Fox moral values. If, in order to get along in the world, a man is required to violate what the group holds necessary and sacred, most will not do it. It is here, for example, that the different notions of authority held by whites and Indians become important. Generally, Indians think it wrong for one man to boss another; white men think legitimate bosses are necessary and good.[2]

The question of change and how it comes about was discussed by a group of social scientists who met in conference at the University of Chicago on February 20, 1954. The immediate subject of discussion was a series of assumptions current in Indian affairs at the time. The most basic of these assumptions, reported to the conference by John Provinse, former Assistant Commissioner of Indian Affairs, was "the idea that assimilation of the American Indian into the normal stream of American life is inevitable, that Indian tribes and communities will disappear."

The conference concluded: "There was complete agreement on the part of the discussants that this prediction is unwarranted. Most Indian groups in the United States, after more than one hundred years of Euro-American contact and in spite of strong external pressures, both direct and fortuitous, have not yet become assimilated in the sense of a loss of community identity and the full acceptance of American habits of thought and conduct. Nor can one expect such group assimilation within any short, predictable time period, say, one to four generations. The urge to retain tribal identity is strong, and operates powerfully for many Indian groups."

The group further concluded that, while individual Indians would doubtless make personal adjustments which would enable them to become incorporated in the general society, "Despite external pressures, and internal change, most of the present identifiable Indian groups residing on reservations (areas long known to them as homelands) will continue indefinitely as distinct social units, preserving their basic values, personality, and Indian way of life, while making continual adjustments, often superficial in nature, to the economic and political demands of the larger society."[3]

The nature of the problem will not yield to law, and resort to legislation at this moment is premature. The concentration of effort should be on bringing into existence among Indians the attitudes and *experiences* which will lead them positively in the directions they select as their goals. If termination of federal trusteeship is a desirable objective of the United States, then let the concentration be on helping Indians to discover reasons why this should be their goal as well.

Indians do not have "manual labor school" minds, as the policy makers once believed. It is not necessary to assume that, unless forced, the Indians will never decide to forgo the government's benevolent protection and accept responsibility for the management of their own affairs. The hesitancy which Indians have displayed in making the decisions which Congress and administrators would like them to make (for the convenience of the United States) grows out of the conditions reported in 1928. The people had neither the training nor the experience to make such decisions, and the deficiencies of 1928 have not yet been removed.

But deficiencies in training and experience are only part of the explanation. The problem has to do with culture and how it operates in men's lives. This element, which is most involved, is most consistently ignored; and as consistently, programs to better the conditions of the Indian people have failed.

Many social scientists have discussed this factor; we quote from a paper by Ruth Benedict on "Recognition of Cultural Diversities in the Postwar World." She is concerned mostly with problems of racial discrimination, but the remarks are appropriate.

The crucial differences which distinguish human societies and human beings are not biological. They are cultural (i.e., they result from learned behavior). . . . This is a truism which is often read off to mean that in a reconstruction program we should provide food that the recipients will accept, or plan houses such as they are accustomed to live in. Of course. But . . . in estimating behavior which is culturally our own as well as in estimating that which is alien to us, we must see it as a historical product, man-made, and inevitably partial. . . .

These cultural patterns are coherent within themselves. . . . This is inevitable, since these cultures are carried by living men and women in their habituated bodies and minds. . . . They hold together, and any one item must be taken in conjunction with the whole structure or it has no relevance. Each item is, as it were, a brick in a total structure; and tearing out the bricks indiscriminately, however inconsequential they seem, may bring the whole structure down in ruins. This does not mean that change is impossible, but that changes have to be adapted to the existing building.[4]

The factor of culture alone explains why Indians and white men, from the first days of European settlement, have never reached a common understanding about land. The policy makers of 1887 attempted to skip over centuries of historical growth by requiring Indians to become private landowners and to acquire the European psychology of individualism. It did not work out in the expected way, yet the policy makers of today still persist.

If an individual Indian owns a piece of land which controls the use of a larger area of adjacent land, the policy makers are encouraging that individual to act in a way that endangers the entire group—probably endangering his own status in the group. He is told that this is "the American way," and therefore the ideal way.

But there is an American way in these matters which is at least as old as the European feudal laws out of which private ownership gradually emerged. This older American way is entitled to work out its own process, which may or may not emerge as private ownership.

In the Indian concept, land is not "real estate." True, it has value; its products can sustain people. But first of all, in the Indian sense, land stands for existence, identity, the place of belonging. This is the significance that Indians are asked to destroy, and understandably they hesitate.

To recapitulate what has been said: since the creation of the Bureau of Indian Affairs in the War Department (1834), the

United States has attempted to ameliorate the conditions in which Indians live. The methods used to achieve this purpose have varied. At times they have canceled each other out, and at other times trends set in motion which might have led to general improvement have been reversed before objectives were reached.

While lack of administrative funds is a chronic condition with the Bureau of Indian Affairs, this has not been the true cause of the failure to bring about improved living conditions. The appropriations from public funds, supplemented by large sums expended out of tribal treasuries, might have sufficed, if money had been the key to the solution to the problem.

Increasingly in recent years the staff employed by the Bureau of Indian Affairs has been professionalized within the civil service, until today most positions in the administrative, management, professional services, and legal branches require college training and even postgraduate training. But a professional staff is effective to the extent that it is trained for a given task, and almost without exception the individuals who have gone to work in the Bureau have not been trained to work in a culture other than their own.

The assumption which has informed the policy of amelioration has been one of insistence on cultural unity. The term used in earlier days was to "civilize" the Indian people; today it is to "integrate" them. The meanings given to these terms in their respective days are approximately the same.

Cultural unity required that the Bureau should provide schools which would teach the standards of white society, hospital and health services which would provide the health care available to white society, farming methods and implements which would turn hunters and primitive agriculturists into efficient farmers. At no point in the development of policy was the question asked: To what extent are Indian children formed by the institutions of their own society before they enter school? Or to what extent do native health concepts create a barrier to the acceptance of scientific medical care? Or by what means is a hunting people motivated to turn to the soil for sustenance, or a primitive subsistence farmer motivated to become a competitive commercial farmer?

It should be obvious that the continuation of a policy which proceeds from an assumption of cultural unity can only have the effect of beating the horse with the same old stick. The remedy lies not in education by itself, though schools are essential and should be available to every Indian child; it is not in better health care, though obviously the physical ills of the Indian people must be dealt with; it is not entirely in the improvement of the economic opportunities of the Indian people, though again better use of resources and better utilization of Indian man power are essential.

None of these factors, together or by themselves, can bring the Indian people from their present condition of isolation in the general society to a condition of full participation as citizens, income producers, and sharers in American life. Achievement of these results is a function of the Indian people. No one can substitute for them. No body of laws and no administrative machinery, however well designed and efficient in operation, can remake the personality of an individual. But the individual, having the desire to help himself, can modulate his life with or without outside help.

The problem then is to devise the conditions and to bring to bear the stimuli which will induce the Indian people to adapt their customs, attitudes, and technical skills to the necessities of life in the American community.

In recent months it has been proposed that a program of technical assistance, based on the so-called Point-4 Program, be established for the Indian people. In fact, legislation to authorize such a program was introduced in the first session of the 85th Congress (Senate Concurrent Resolution 3); hearings were held at which a number of tribal delegates testified favorably, but no final action was taken.

The language stating the purpose of the resolution is of particular interest since, if adopted, it would wipe out the termination policy—what *The New York Times* on July 20, 1958, characterized as a "blot" on the administration and on Congress.

The pertinent language reads:

It is declared to be the sense of Congress that this program shall be offered to the American Indian communities without exacting termination of federal protection of Indian property or of any other Indian rights as its price; that Indian culture and identity shall not be restricted or destroyed; that technical guidance and financial assistance shall be made available; that the request for assistance shall come from the Indians themselves after each Indian group has studied itself in terms of its own needs; that an impartial effort shall be made to deal with the development of natural resources to maximum capacity, to develop the full capabilities of industrial and agricultural production, of improvements in housing, nutrition, clothing, sanitation, and health, and of the resettlement on the initiative of individuals and families in other areas; that technical assistance shall be given to long term general, vocational, technical, and professional education to enable American Indians to share fully in our total American society and to contribute to it; and that older, revered values shall be respected and used as new forms of living are introduced.

In reporting on this proposal, the Under Secretary of the Interior, Hatfield Chilson, offered statements which, if they are to be charitably explained, suggest that he was not familiar with the Point 4 Program and perhaps even less familiar with current operations of the Bureau of Indian Affairs. In objecting to the legislation, he stated: "We think that the application of the Point-4 concept to the Indian program would be unfortunate in two respects: first, because it implies that the government has not been providing similar services for the Indian people; and second, because it tends to restrict the present Indian program to the type of technical and economic assistance provided to foreign governments, which is much more limited than the presently authorized program for Indians."

There is a fundamental difference between the programs operated by the United States in behalf of the Indian people and the technical assistance programs commonly referred to as Point 4. It is just this: the United States decides what programs should be initiated on an Indian reservation; it alone determines how much shall be expended, how long it will continue, and when it shall terminate. It employs the personnel, establishes the qualifications of those employed, and at all times is in full control of operations. If Indians are consulted at all, it is a formality, and their opinions can have no deciding effect, since a federal program need not have their approval and they are not required to pay any part of the cost.

In contrast, a Point 4 Program is not undertaken unless the people of a country request it. Within the limits of its financial ability, the requesting country must share the cost in money, goods, or services. Management is jointly shared, with the requesting country having full authority to veto any items within a proposal; and operations are carried out through existing agencies and facilities of the requesting country.

But it is the operating method of Point 4 programs which has greatest significance for the administration of Indian affairs in this country. The Meriam survey report had made the emphatic plea that "the task of the Indian Service be recognized as primarily educational in the broadest sense of the word, and that it be made an efficient educational agency, devoting its main energies to the social and economic advancement of the Indians. . . ."

This is exactly the operating philosophy of Point 4 programs, as described by William E. Warne, formerly Assistant Secretary of the Interior, later director of the Point 4 Program in Iran. In *Mission for Peace*, Warne describes how a program operates:

It would have a life of five years. The first year would be spent in preparation—training Iranian technicians, locating sites and importing the required tools and equipment. During the second year the newly trained Iranian technicians would launch the field work and demonstration projects, working through the agency sponsoring the project. Activity would reach its peak in the third year. The American technicians, the Iranian technicians and all cooperators would then be putting every ounce of energy into the operation of the project. In the fourth year the American technicians would turn their responsibilities over to their Iranian counterparts. And in the fifth year the Iranians would conduct project activities with little or no assistance, except for occasional consultation or advice, from the American technicians. . . .

The whole technical cooperation program, however, was never designed for a five year life. The program in Iran was conceived as a continuous rope pulling that country forward. The rope was to be made up of strands of projects, each five years long. These projects would be intertwined to make a single program for the improvement of the life of the people. New strands will be woven in as the ends of old ones are reached. It is long range.[5]

Mr. Chilson's statement that the Indian Service offers a more complete program than Point 4 is equally inexact. The agreement with Iran, for example, included assistance in health and sanitation, education and training, student assistance, industry, sugar importation, transportation, community housing, natural resources development, communications, land distribution, public administration, agrarian development, and land reform. In any given country, this list of activities might be shorter or longer; it would depend on the needs of the people and what they were ready to undertake. Under present policy, the Indians of the United States do not have the privilege of specifying their needs. That is accomplished for them by technical men, employed to assist them, who, in reality, obstruct and defeat them.

Whether or not the proposal submitted as Senate Concurrent Resolution 3 in the 85th Congress is the form in which assistance can best be offered to the Indians is something that the Indians should decide for themselves. Congress has the plenary power, it can make the decision; but if it does so, to the exclusion of Indian participation, it will only continue the tradition of the "compulsory process." In acknowledgment of the mistakes of the past, the tradition ought to be finally denounced. Rescinding Concurrent Resolution 108 of the 83rd Congress would clear the way.

The unfulfilled dream of the Indians of this country is that they will be permitted at last to make the primary decisions affecting their lives and their property. Not that their decisions will be superior to those made by men possibly more skillful; but that, being their decisions, the people will be content to live with them and to change them as experience teaches the desirability of change.

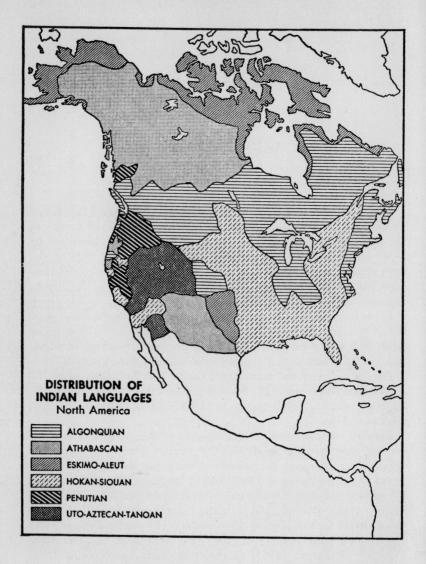

DISTRIBUTION OF INDIAN LANGUAGES
North America

	ALGONQUIAN
	ATHABASCAN
	ESKIMO-ALEUT
	HOKAN-SIOUAN
	PENUTIAN
	UTO-AZTECAN-TANOAN

APPENDIX

Indian Languages

The complexity of Indian occupation in the New World is revealed by the study of Indian languages, of which about 150 still survive in the area north of Mexico. The system of classification developed by J. W. Powell in 1891 was revised by Edward Sapir in 1929 on the basis of later and more complete information. By indicating relationships based on internal structure, Sapir was able to group the fifty-six linguistic stocks of Powell's classification into six major language types.

In the following listing, the numerals indicate the approximate number of persons who speak languages belonging to one of these major types. The arrangement also suggests a possible chronology of migration, from the earliest to the most recent, adopted from Voegelin.[1]

The six types of the Sapir classification are: I, Eskimo-Aleut; II, Algonquian-Wakashan; III, Na-dene; IV, Uto-Aztecan-Tanoan; V, Penutian; and VI, Hokan-Siouan. In ascending time order, the arrangement would be:

Type VI, Hokan-Siouan. The languages of this group represent the greatest geographical spread, also the greatest diversity of form. The area is not continuous, but consists of numerous large and small segments of territory separated by intruding languages. The range is from the eastern seaboard (Catawba and other Siouan people) to California (Karok, Pomo, Washo), and from the Canadian border (the Iroquois tribes) to the Gulf of Mexico (Chitimacha). The principal extant tribes are Iroquois (Six Nations) in New York, Wisconsin, and Oklahoma (12,000); Tuscarora (500); Cherokee in North Carolina and Oklahoma (50,000); Choctaw in Mississippi and Oklahoma (22,000); Chickasaw (5,500); Creek (10,000); Caddo (1,200); Pawnee (1,150); Arikara (700); Dakota (42,000); Crow (3,000); Osage

(4,600); Quapaw (650); Winnebago (3,000); Mandan (400); Hidatsa (850); Washo (520); Pomo (860); Havasupai, Walapai, Yavapai (1,300); Mohave, Yuma, Maricopa, etc. (2,300); Digueno (Mission), (7,000).

Type V, Penutian. The geographical spread of this language type is confined to a relatively limited area extending from north central California to southeastern Alaska and British Columbia, but evidently it has linguistic components in Central America. The group is characterized by many small tribes, some of which are now extinct or have lost identity. The principal tribes are Maidu (170); Miwok (490); Wintun (500); Klamath-Modoc (2,000); Yokuts (1,145); Sahaptin, which includes Tenino, Wallawalla, Umatilla, Yakima, and Nez Percé (6,500); Chinook (600); and Tsimshian (700).

Type II, Algonquian-Wakashan. The distribution of this group is from Nova Scotia and New Brunswick across the continent to Vancouver Island, and from Hudson Bay southward to Ohio and the upper Mississippi Valley. The more prominent tribes are Cree (10,000 mostly in Canada), Menominee (2,550), Sauk and Fox (1,600), Shawnee (750), Potawatomi (3,500), Ojibway (32,000), Penobscot (250), Passamaquoddy (400), Blackfeet (5,000), Arapaho (2,200), Cheyenne (3,500), Yurok (1,000), Kutenai (1,000), Makah (450), Salish (Coastal and Interior), (16,000). See *Algonquian* on accompanying map.

Type IV, Uto-Aztecan-Tanoan. The geographical area is roughly the high plateau area and Great Basin west of the Rocky Mountains, with extensions into the valley of Mexico, and perhaps into Middle America. Best known of the tribes are Pima and Papago (14,000), Hopi (3,700), Ute and Paiute (5,800), Shoshone (3,700), Comanche (2,700), Rio Grande pueblos (Keresan, Tewa, and Tiwa, 12,000), Kiowa (2,700), and Zuni (2,500).

Type III, Na-dene [Athabascan]. This group includes Apache tribes in Arizona and New Mexico (6,500), the numerous Navajo tribe (80,000), the Tlingit (4,000) and Haida (1,000) of southeastern Alaska, the Hupa (700) and several small tribes in California, and a score of northern tribes inhabiting the region between Alaska and Hudson Bay and from the Canadian border to the Arctic slope. The line of distribution is a north-south one extending over several thousand miles. See *Athabascan* on accompanying map.

Type I, Eskimo-Aleut. This type represents the least diversity, the speech of the Kuskokwim Eskimos varying but slightly from their Greenland kinsmen, and that of the Aleutian Islanders diverging still further. They occupy a continuous geographic area, except where open water intervenes, from Siberia to Greenland. The total population is estimated at 50,000.

NOTES

Chapter I

1. Francis E. Leupp, *The Indian and His Problem* (New York, 1910).
2. The policy is stated in House Concurrent Resolution 108, 83rd Congress, 1st Session (1953).

Chapter II

1. Indian population studies: James Mooney, "The Aboriginal Population of America North of Mexico" (revised by John R. Swanton), Smithsonian Institution, *Miscellaneous Collections,* Vol. 80 (Washington, 1928); A. L. Kroeber, *Cultural and Natural Areas of Native North America* (Berkeley, 1939).
2. Sol Tax, with collaboration of Robert Thomas and Samuel Stanley, "The Present Day Distribution of United States Indians," paper read at 55th Annual Meeting, American Anthropological Association (1956).
3. Richard Hakluyt, in Samuel Purchas' *Pilgrims* (1625).
4. The archaeological record is reviewed by H. M. Wormington, *Ancient Man in North America,* Denver Museum of Natural History (Denver, 1957). Specific aspects are presented in individual papers published in Smithsonian Institution, *Miscellaneous Collections,* Vol. 100 (Washington, 1940), and American Philosophical Society, *Proceedings,* Vol. 86, No. 2 (Philadelphia, 1943).
    Physical characteristics are analyzed by E. A. Hooton, "Racial Types in America and their Relation to Old World Types," in *The American Aborigines,* Diamond Jenness, ed. (Toronto, 1933).
    Correlation of physical type and possible sequence of migration: Harold S. Gladwin, "Excavations at Snaketown II: Comparisons and Theories," *Medallion Papers,* No. 26 (Globe, Ariz., 1937).
    Language distribution as a clue to sequence of migration is offered by C. F. Voegelin, "Relative Chronology of North American Linguistic Types," *American Anthropologist,* Vol. 47, No. 2 (1945).
    Distribution of aboriginal population is taken from Kroeber, *Cultural and Natural Areas.*

Chapter III

1. For a good account of the manner in which complex European land concepts were transplanted to the New World, see William B. Munro, "The Seigniorial System in Canada, A Study in French Colonial Policy," *Harvard Historical Studies*, XIII (New York, 1907).
2. Land tenure among American aborigines has extensive bibliography. See Frank G. Speck, "Land Ownership Among Hunting Peoples in Primitive America and the World's Marginal Areas," in *22nd International Congress of Americanists* (1926); John M. Cooper, "The Culture of the Northeastern Indian Hunters," *Papers of the R S. Peabody Foundation for Archaeology*, Vol. 3 (1946); A. Irving Hallowell, "The Size of the Algonkian Hunting Territory: A Function of Ecological Adjustment," *American Anthropologist*, Vol. 51, No. 1 (1949). For nonhunting societies, see Fred Eggan, *Social Organization of the Western Pueblos* (Chicago, 1950), and references.
3. The petition offered by the Five Civilized Tribes is found in the *Congressional Record*, 46th Cong., 3rd Sess., Vol. XI, Part 1, p. 781.
4. Johnson's and Graham's Lessee *v.* McIntosh, 8 Wheaton 543 (1823).
5. See "A Bibliography on the Agriculture of the American Indians," compiled by Everett E. Edwards and Wayne D. Rasmussen, U.S. Department of Agriculture, *Miscellaneous Publications*, No. 447 (1942).
6. The Cherokee story has been told many times. See Ralph Henry Gabriel, *Elias Boudinot, Cherokee, and His America* (Norman, Okla., 1941).
7. Senator Frelinghuysen's speech is published in Thomas H. Benton's *Abridgement of the Debates in Congress, 1789–1865* (Washington, 1859) Vol. X, pp. 519–25.

Chapter IV

1. Carl L. Becker, *Progress and Power* (Stanford, 1936).
2. Roy Harvey Pearce, *The Savages of America* (Baltimore, 1953).
3. Arthur A. Ekirch, *The Idea of Progress in America, 1815–1860* (New York, 1944).
4. Helen Hunt Jackson, *A Century of Dishonor* (New York, 1881).
5. Conners *v.* U. S., 33 Court of Claims 317 (1898).

Chapter V

1. This possible cultural sequence is discussed in Gladwin, "Excavations at Snaketown II"; E. B. Sayles and Ernst Antevs, "The Cochise Culture," *Medallion Papers*, No. 24 (Globe, Ariz., 1941); Emil

Haury and collaborators, *The Stratigraphy and Archaeology of Ventana Cave, Arizona* (Albuquerque, 1950); Paul C. Mangelsdorf and E. Earle Smith, Jr., "New Archaeological Evidence on Evolution in Maize," *Botanical Leaflets*, Harvard University, Vol. 13, No. 6 (Cambridge, 1949).

2. Much of the historical record of government relations with the Pima Indians is drawn from Indian Bureau files. See also, Frank Russell, "The Pima Indians," Bureau of American Ethnology, *26th Annual Report*, Smithsonian Institution (Washington, 1904–5).

3. The Coolidge Dam Act, June 7, 1924 (43 Stat. 475). Italics supplied.

Chapter VI

1. The Marshall opinion is quoted from Worcester *v.* Georgia, 6 Peters 515 (1832).

2. The Walker statement is contained in the *Commissioner's Annual Report* for 1872.

3. The Dutch policy is quoted in C. C. Royce, "Indian Land Cessions in the United States," *18th Annual Report*, Part 2, Bureau of American Ethnology (Washington, 1902).

4. The instructions to Captain Endecott are given in Alexander Young, *Chronicles of the First Planters of the Colony of Massachusetts Bay, 1623–1636* (Boston, 1846).

5. For William Penn's transactions, see Royce, "Indian Land Cessions."

6. Woolman's *Journal* was originally published in 1774. It was edited and reissued by John Greenleaf Whittier in 1871.

7. Helen Louise Shaw, "British Administration of the Southern Indians, 1756–1783" (Ph.D. Thesis, Bryn Mawr College, 1931).

8. Wilbur R. Jacobs, ed., *Indians of the Southern Colonial Frontier, the Edmund Atkin Report and Plan of 1755* (Chapel Hill, N.C., 1954).

9. Clarence W. Alvord, "The Genesis of the Proclamation of 1763," *Michigan Pioneer and Historical Collection*, Vol. 36 (Lansing, 1908).

10. See *Journals of the Continental Congress*, ed. Worthington C. Ford, Gaillard Hunt, J. C. Fitzpatrick, and R. R. Hill (Washington, 1904–37).

11. For Knox's views, see American State Papers, Class II, *Indian Affairs*, Vol. I.

12. Johnson's and Graham's Lessee *v.* McIntosh, 8 Wheaton 543 (1823); Cherokee Nation *v.* Georgia, 5 Peters 1 (1831); Worcester *v.* Georgia, 6 Peters 515 (1832).

13. United States *v.* Shoshone Tribe, 304 U.S. 111 (1938), affirming decision in 85 Ct. Clms. 331 (1937).
14. United States as Guardian of Hualapai *v.* Santa Fe Pacific Railroad Co., 314 U.S. 339 (1941).

Chapter VII

1. The Jackson letter to Monroe is given in *Correspondence of Andrew Jackson,* ed. John S. Bassett (Washington, 1926–35), Vol. II, pp. 277–82.
2. *Ibid.,* p. 331.
3. Alexis de Tocqueville, *Democracy in America,* trans. Henry Reeves (New York, 1898).

Chapter VIII

1. The material for this chapter is drawn principally from the following sources: *Annual Reports* of the Commissioner of Indian Affairs, 1825 to date (after 1934 the Commissioner's report appears as part of the *Annual Report* of the Secretary of the Interior); Laurence F. Schmeckebier, *The Office of Indian Affairs* (Baltimore, 1927); Felix S. Cohen, *Handbook of Federal Indian Law* (Washington, 1945); official files, Bureau of Indian Affairs.

Chapter IX

1. The Massachusetts act of 1633 and the statement by John Winthrop are quoted in Royce, "Indian Land Cessions."
2. The history of events resulting in the adoption of the allotment law, and its immediate consequences, are provided by D. S. Otis, "History of the Allotment Policy," in *Hearings Before the Committee on Indian Affairs, House of Representatives,* 73rd Cong., 2nd Sess. on H.R. 7902 (Washington, 1934).
3. Senator Teller's remarks and related debates are found in the *Congressional Record,* 46th Cong., 3rd Sess., Vol. XI, June 20, 1881.
4. The minority committee report is in House Report No. 1576, 46th Cong., 2nd Sess., May 28, 1880.
5. The Dawes statement is quoted in Otis, "History of the Allotment Policy."
6. Land losses resulting from allotment law procedures were compiled by the National Resources Board and published in "Indian Land Tenure, Economic Status, and Population Trends," *Supplementary Report of the Land Planning Committee* (Washington, 1935), Part X.
7. Gordon Macgregor, *Warriors Without Weapons* (Chicago, 1946).

8. For the Sisseton record, see D'Arcy McNickle, "Rescuing Sisseton," *The American Indian*, Vol. III, No. 2 (1946).
9. Collier's statement is reported in the *Hearings* on H.R. 7902.
10. The statement of Indian attitude is in *Report of the Commissioner of Indian Affairs* (1887), p. 117.

Chapter X

1. The investigation is reported in *Fifty-Second Annual Report of the Board of Indian Commissioners* (1921).
2. A good account of this period is Randolph C. Downes "A Crusade for Reform, 1922–1934," *Mississippi Valley Historical Review*, Vol. XXXII, No. 3, 1945.
3. Lewis Meriam and associates, *The Problem of Indian Administration* (Baltimore, 1928).
4. Commissioner's *Annual Report*, 1931.

Chapter XI

1. Act of May 21, 1934 (48 Stat. 787).
2. The citizenship status of Indians is analyzed at length in Cohen, *Handbook of Federal Indian Law*, Chapter 8, "Personal Rights and Liberties of Indians."
3. Act of June 18, 1934 (48 Stat. 984).
4. The petition is recited in full in "Speech of Hon. William H. King," *Senate Document, No. 214*, 72nd Cong., 2nd Sess., 1933.
5. This report was incorporated, with some revisions, as Chapter 7, "The Scope of Tribal Self-Government," in Cohen, *Handbook of Federal Indian Law*.
6. The figures on land purchases, credit operations, land use, and income are taken from the Commissioner's *Annual Reports* for the years noted.
7. The statement of purpose of the applied anthropology unit is from Bureau of Indian Affairs files.
8. Act of April 16, 1934 (48 Stat. 596).
9. Act of August 8, 1946 (6 Stat. 939).
10. Act of August 13, 1946 (60 Stat. 1049).

Chapter XII

1. Considerable historical material and evaluations of Indian education programs are offered by Evelyn C. Adams, *American Indian Education* (New York, 1946), and Lloyd E. Blauch, "Educational Service for Indians," Advisory Committee on Education, *Staff Study No. 18* (Washington, 1939). See also Willard W. Beatty, *Education for Action*, U.S. Indian Service Publication (1944), for articles on school methods, policies, etc.

2. The statement is found in Adams, *American Indian Education*.
3. For comment on the recommendations of the Committee of One Hundred, see Downes, "A Crusade for Reform," Chapter X.
4. The report of the National Advisory Committee on Education is summarized in Blauch, "Educational Service for Indians."
5. Dr. Shailer Peterson, *How Well Are Indian Children Educated?* U.S. Indian Service Publication (1948).
6. The comparative intelligence-test findings are published in Robert J. Havighurst and Rhea R. Hilkevitch, "The Intelligence of Indian Children as Measured by a Performance Scale," *Journal of Abnormal and Social Psychology*, Vol. 39 (1944), and Havighurst, Minna Korol, and Inez E. Pratt, "Environment and the Draw-a-Man Test: The Performance of Indian Children," *ibid.*, Vol. 40 (1946). For a more incisive study of cultural contrasts in emotional relationships, values and aversions, and basic moral attitudes, see Havighurst and Bernice L. Neugarten, *American Indian and White Children* (Chicago, 1955).

Chapter XIII

1. Mitchell *v.* U.S., 9 Peters 711 (1835).
2. The quotation is from a memorandum of August 2, 1952, directed to "All Bureau Officials."
3. The recommendations on land needs are noted above (Chapter 9), in the report of the National Resources Board.
4. Act of May 1, 1936 (49 Stat. 1250).
5. The Alaska reservations are cited in the *Annual Report*, Bureau of Indian Affairs (1944).
6. Senate Joint Resolution 162 and S. 2037, 80th Cong., 2nd Sess. (1948). The letter of the Acting Comptroller General is contained in the Hearings on the above proposals.

Chapter XIV

1. Act of July 1, 1932 (47 Stat. 564).
2. Act of May 31, 1933 (48 Stat. 108).
3. Act of May 11, 1938 (52 Stat. 347).
4. The revised leasing and individual money regulations are explained in the Bureau's *Annual Report* for 1948.
5. The circular of November 15, 1943, is in Bureau files.
6. The *Annual Report* for 1947 refers to this testimony.

Chapter XV

1. For our "lawless heritage," see James Truslow Adams, *Our Business Civilization* (New York, 1929).
2. Information about the Klamath reservation and people is given in

Joint Hearings Before the Subcommittees of the Committees on Interior and Insular Affairs. . . , 83rd Cong., 2nd Sess., on S. 2745 and H.R. 7320, Part 4 and Part 4-a (Washington, 1954).

3. Verne F. Ray, "The Klamath Oppose Liquidation," *The American Indian,* Vol. IV, No. 4 (1948).

4. *Joint Hearings.*

5. The appraisal of tribal assets and results of the referendum are quoted in *The New York Times,* April 29, 1958.

Chapter XVI

1. See *Annual Report* for 1931 on establishment of placement service.

2. Myer's views were presented in "Address by Dillon S. Myer, Before . . . the National Council of Churches of Christ," Buck Hill Falls, Pennsylvania, December 12, 1951.

3. The comment on extension work is from the *Annual Report,* 1938.

4. The problems faced by Indians moving into urban areas have been reported on in various studies. See *The Reservation Indian Comes to Town* (New York, 1953); *The American Indian Relocation Program* (New York, 1956); and *The Minnesota Indian in Minneapolis* (Minneapolis, 1956).

Chapter XVII

1. Data on the Turtle Mountain reservation and people are provided in *Joint Hearings . . . on S. 2748 and H. R. 7316,* 83rd Cong., 2nd Sess., Part 12 (March 2–3, 1954).

2. Discussion of Public Law 280 in *Proceedings of the Conference on Indian Tribes and Treaties,* University of Minnesota, April 24–28, 1956, pp. 50–51 and 132–140.

3. "Indian Land Transactions," *Memorandum of the Chairman to the Committee on Interior and Insular Affairs,* United States Senate, 85th Congress, 2nd Session, Washington, December 1, 1958.

4. A resolution adopted by the National Congress of American Indians at its 13th Annual Convention (Salt Lake City, September 24–28, 1956) requested that the tribal governing body of each reservation be accorded "a prior right and opportunity to purchase."

5. W. O. Roberts, "The Vanishing Homeland," in *Indian Affairs,* newsletter of the Association on American Indian Affairs, January, 1957.

6. For a recent history of the Cherokees, see Marion L. Starkey, *The Cherokee Nation* (New York, 1946).

Chapter XVIII

1. For Navajo history, see Edward T. Hall, Jr., "Recent Clues to Athapascan Prehistory in the Southwest," *American Anthropologist,*

Vol. 46, No. 1 (1944); W. W. Hill, "Some Navajo Cultural Changes During Two Centuries," Smithsonian Institution, *Miscellaneous Collections,* Vol. 100 (1940). For contemporary Navajo culture, see Clyde Kluckhohn and Dorothea Leighton, *The Navajo* (Cambridge, Mass., 1948).

2. For the growth of livestock industry, see Robert W. Young, *The Navajo Yearbook* (Window Rock, Ariz., 1955), and Bureau files.
3. Testimony before Senate Committee on Indian Affairs, 79th Cong., 2nd Sess., on S.J. Res. 79 (1946).
4. Allan G. Harper, "Navajo Education," *The American Indian,* Vol. V, No. 4 (New York, 1950).
5. John Adair, "The Navajo and Pueblo Veteran," *The American Indian,* Vol. IV, No. 1 (New York, 1947).
6. *The Navajo,* report of J. A. Krug, Secretary of the Interior (Washington, March, 1948).
7. Act of April 1, 1950 (64 Stat. 44).

Chapter XIX

1. House of Representatives, 83rd Cong., 2nd Sess., Union Calendar No. 925, Report No. 2680 (September 20, 1954).
2. Sol Tax, Fred Gearing, and Robert Rietz, "Symposium: The Fox Project," annual meeting of the Central States Anthropological Society, 1956.
3. John Provinse and others, "The American Indian in Transition," Wenner-Gren Conference, *American Anthropologist,* Vol. 56, No. 3 (1954).
4. Ruth Benedict, "Recognition of Cultural Diversities in the Postwar World," *Annals,* American Academy of Political and Social Science (July 1943).
5. William E. Warne, *Mission for Peace* (New York, 1956).

Appendix

1. C. F. Voegelin, "Relative Chronology of North American Linguistic Types," *American Anthropologist,* Vol. 47, No. 2 (1945).

INDEX

Adair, John, 183–84
Agriculture, 24, 26, 29–30, 38–39, 101, 176
Agriculture Department, 101, 104, 177
Alaska, 125–28
Albany Congress (1754), 50
Algonquian-Wakashan language group, 23, 204
Allen, Henry E., 163–64
All-Pueblo Council, 83
American Ethnology, Bureau of, 102
American Indian Development, 188
American Legion, 169
American Red Cross, 115
Anthropology, applied, unit of, 102
Apache Indians, 175
Arizona Republic, 45
Army, U.S., 35–37, 176, 185
Arthur Scale, 118
Asheville Citizen, 171
Asia, 22
Assiniboine Indians, 22
Athabascan tribes, 175
Atkin, Edmund, 50–51
Atlantis, 22

Baldwin, Roger N., 94
Bapchule district, Ariz., 45
Barkley, Rev. Thomas, 109
Bat Cave, Ariz., 39
Beatty, Willard W., 118
Becker, Carl L., 32–33
Bellemont, Ariz., 183
Benedict, Ruth, 194–95
Bering Strait, 22
Berkeley, Calif., 149
Black Horse (Navajo), 182
Board of Trade, 50
Boas, Franz, 94
Boston, Mass., 52
Boudinot, Elias (Cherokee), 30
Bourke, Captain, 36

Braddock, Maj. Gen. Edward, 49, 50
Broad-headedness, 22
Brookings Institution, 83
Budget Bureau, 180
Burleson, Bishop Hugh L., 94
Bursum bill (1922), 83

Calhoun, John C., 62
Calvert family, 26, 27
Carlisle, Pa., 110
Carson, Kit, 176
Cass, Lewis, 64
Catawba Indians, 19
Census Bureau, 18, 19
Century of Dishonor, A (Jackson), 35
Chemawa, Ore., 110
Cherokee Historical Association, 170
Cherokee Indians, 30–31, 32, 93, 109, 123, 168–73
Cherokee Nation v. Georgia (1831), 54, 91
Cherokee Tribal Fair, 171
Cheyenne Indians, 35–37
Chicago, Ill., 45–46
Chicago, University of, 19, 117, 193
Chicago Sun-Times, 46
Chickasaw Indians, 93, 109
Chilocco, Indian Territory, 110
Chilson, Hatfield, 198, 200
Chippewa Indians, 153, 158–61
Chitimacha Indians, 22
Chivington, Col. J. M., 35
Choctaw Academy, 109–10
Choctaw Indians, 19, 59, 93, 109
Civil Air Patrol, 185
Civil Service Commission, 117
Civil War, 35, 71, 105
Civilian Conservation Corps, 101
Claims Commission Act (1946), 104–5
Cleveland, Grover, 73
Cochise culture, 38–39

Code of Indian Offenses, 162
Cohen, Felix S., 97
Coke, Richard, 73
Collier, John, 78, 99, 101, 131–33
Colorado River Indian Reservation
    185
Columbus, Christopher, 17, 25
Committee of One Hundred, 112
Community Welfare Council, Min
    neapolis, 153–55
Confederate states, 105
Congress, 15, 27, 31, 40, 43, 46, 59
    63, 67, 78, 88, 90, 95, 97, 99
    103, 106, 108, 111, 116, 120
    126, 127, 132 ff., 148, 151–52
    161 ff., 184 ff., 191, 192, 194
    197–98, 200
    and General Allotment Act, 72–7
    and Klamath tribe, 139–47
    and Sand Creek massacre, 35–36
    and treaties, 91–92
Connors v. *U.S.*, 36–37
Constitution, 58, 91
Continental Congress, 52, 107–8
Coolidge Dam, 40–43
Court of Claims, U.S., 36–37, 105
Crawford, T. Hartley, 65
Creek Indians, 93, 109
Crook, Maj. Gen. George, 36
Crownpoint, N. Mex., 187–88

Dances, 14
Dartmouth College, 107–8
Davenport, Charles C., 94
Dawes, Henry L., 73–74
Delaware Indians, 49, 108
Denver, James W., 66
Department of Indian Affairs, 14
Depressions, 76–77, 115
Descent, lines of, 20
Diseases, 17
Dodge, Chee, 180
Duane, James, 52
Dull Knife (Cheyenne), 36
Dutch East India Company, 49
Dutch West India Company, 49

East India Company, 49

Eastern Band of Cherokee Indians,
    168
Education, 65, 71, 80, 85, 89, 96,
    196–97
    background, 107–12
    Navajo Indians, 181–83
    reforms, 113–19
Egypt, 22
Eisenhower, Dwight D., 162
Ekirch, Arthur A., 34
Eliot, John, 107
Emmons, Glenn L., 166, 172
Employment, 97, 148–57
Endecott, Capt. John, 48
Engineers, Army, 40
Eskimo-Aleut language group, 23,
    204–5
Eskimos, 24, 125
European Recovery Program, 187

Fishing, 23
Five Civilized Tribes, 27, 109
Fort Defiance, Ariz., 176, 182
Fort Leavenworth, Kans., 110
Fort Lyon, Colo., 35
Fort Robinson, Wyo., 36–37
Fort Sumner, N. Mex., 176, 178
Fort Wingate, N. Mex., 183
Fox Indians, 192–93
France, 49, 51, 63
Frelinghuysen, Theodore, 31
Fur trapping, 27, 125

General Allotment Act (1887), 67,
    70, 72–75, 78, 81, 93, 138, 190,
    192
General Land Office, 55
Genoa, Neb., 110
Geological Survey, U.S., 40
Georgia, University of, 171
Gila River, 38–43, 75
"Gila River Decree," 41
Goodenough "Draw-a-Man" tests,
    118
Grace Arthur Point Performance
    Scale, 118
Great Britain, relations with Indians,
    49–51, 63, 107
Great Plains Committee, 104, 123

Great Smoky Mountains National Park, 169
Green, Paul, 170
Guam, 114

Hale, Edward Everett, 73–74
Harper, Allan G., 182–83
Haskell Institute, 110, 112
Haverford College, 171
Hayes, Ira, 44–46
Haynes, John R., 94
Hayt, Ezra A., 72
Henry, Patrick, 52
Hillman, Arthur, 156
Hokan-Siouan language group, 22–23, 203–4
Homestead Act (1862), 71
Hopi Indians, 118, 174, 184–86
House of Representatives, 59, 63, 73, 135–36, 180
    Committee on Indian Affairs, 95, 141, 163, 192
Howard, Edgar, 95
Hualapai Indians, 55–56
Hunter, Kermit, 170
Hunting, 27, 30, 39, 121, 175
Hutchins, Robert M., 94

Indian Affairs, Bureau of, 18, 19, 40, 43, 45, 61–62, 101, 103–4, 125, 159, 165, 177, 195–96
    Commissioner, 39–40, 48, 61–62, 65–69, 86, 88–90, 92, 103–4, 116, 122, 133 ff., 149, 165–67
    and education, 110–19
    investigation of, 133–36
    relocation program, 148–57, 158–61
    superintendents, 103, 168–72
Indian Affairs Commission, 160
Indian Claims Commission, 104–6
Indian Commissioners, Board of, 81–82
Indian Department, 53
Indian Removal Act (1830), 31, 59, 92, 189
Indian Reorganization Act (1934), 68, 93–101, 121 ff., 129, 130, 132, 133, 140, 158, 162 ff., 191

Indian Territory, 36, 110
Indians, and change, 193–94
    citizenship, 93, 137
    and culture, 194–97
    education, see Education
    and European social attitudes, 32–37, 48–51
    government relations, 47–56, 61–69, 91–106, 120–37, 189–92
        Klamath tribe, 139–47
    health, 84, 85, 101, 196–97
    land tenure, 26–31, 39–44, 54 ff., 57–59, 65–66, 68, 70–79, 80–84, 90, 93, 96, 99–100, 116, 121 ff., 159, 164–67, 195
    languages, see Languages
    migration to New World, 20–22
    need for change, 13–16
    origin, 21–22
    population, 17–19, 23, 93–94, 176, 203–5
    relocation program, 148–57, 158–61
    reservations, see Reservations
    technical-assistance program, 197–200
    termination measures, 139–47, 158–61
    tribes, constitutions of, 98, 186
        powers of, 97–98
        territorial system, 26–27
Institute for Government Research, 68, 83
Intelligence tests, 117–18
Interior Department, 37, 40, 41, 43, 55, 59, 62, 96–97, 100, 102–3, 104, 125, 128, 136, 144, 160, 180
International Harvester Company, 45
Iran, 199–200
Iroquois Confederacy, 93
Iroquois Indians, 22, 52
Irrigation, 39–44, 46
Israel, lost tribe of, 22
Iwo Jima, 14, 44, 45

Jackson, Andrew, 31, 32, 57–59, 122
Jackson, Boyd, 141–43
Jackson, Helen Hunt, 35, 36

Japanese–Americans, relocation of, 151

Jennings, Joe, 168–69, 171, 172

Johnson, Col. Richard M., 109

Johnson, Sir William, 50

Johnson-O'Malley Act (1934), 102

Johnson's and Graham's Lessee v. *McIntosh* (1823), 54

Justice Department, 105

Kansas City, 149

Karok Indians, 22

Kaskaskia Indians, 108

King, William H., 90, 115–16, 122

Kino, Father E. F., 39

Kinship systems, 20

Kirk, Seldon, 144–45

Klamath Indians, 14, 139–47, 189, 192

Klamath Termination Act (1954), 143, 158, 161

Knox, Henry, 53–54

Languages, 20, 22–23, 26, 30, 47, 179

types, classification of, 203–5

Law of Nations (Vattel), 30

Lawrence, Kans., 110

Leavitt Act (1932), 129–30

Leupp, Francis E., 13–14, 68–69

Little Wolf (Cheyenne), 36

Livestock, Navajo Indians, 176–79

Livingston, Philip, 52

Long-headedness, 22

Los Alamos, N. Mex., 183

Los Angeles, Calif., 46, 149

McKenney, Thomas L., 62, 65, 71

Manypenny, George W., 65–66

Margold, Nathan R., 97

Marine Corps, 179

Marshall, George C., 184

Marshall, John, 28–29, 31, 47–48, 54–55, 57, 91

Massachusetts Bay Company, 48

Massachusetts General Court, 70–71

Menominee Indians, 139, 140, 189

Meriam, Lewis, survey and report of, 68, 83–88, 93, 94, 101, 102, 113–15, 116, 117, 121 ff., 129, 190–91, 199

Methodist Church, 110

Mexican Springs grazing unit, 104

Mexico, 39

Minneapolis, Minn., 149, 153–56

Fair Practices Commission, 155

Health Department, 155

Minnesota, University of, Center for Continuation Study, 163

Minnesota Indian in Minneapolis, The, 153

Mission for Peace (Warne), 199–200

Missionaries, 14, 30, 32, 108–10

Mitchell v. *United States* (1835), 120

Mohawk Indians, 109

Monroe, James, 57–59, 108, 121, 141

Moor's Charity School, 107

Morgan, Thomas J., 67–68, 80, 111

Morgan, Lewis H., 34

Myer, Dillon S., 122, 135–36, 150–51, 152, 156

Na-dene language group, 23, 204

National Advisory Committee on Education, 114–15

National Congress of American Indians, 191

National Guard, 185

National Park Service, 169

National Resources Board, 104, 123, 124, 149

Navajo Agency, 184

Navajo Indians, 47, 104, 118, 174–88

New Deal, 92

New England Indians, 17

New Netherland, 48

New York Times, 197–98

Niza, Fray Marcos de, 38–39

North Carolina, University of, 170, 171

Northwest Ordinance (1787), 57, 63

Oberly, John H., 111

Old Crow (Cheyenne), 36

Oneida Indians, 52, 108

Ordinance for the Government of the Northwest Territory (1787), 53

Ordinance for the Regulation of Indian Affairs (1786), 53
Osage Indians, 139
Otoe and Missouri case, 105

Papago Indians, 38, 118
Parker, Ely S., 66–67
Peabody, George Foster, 94
Pearce, Roy Harvey, 34
Penn, William, 26, 27, 49
Penutian language group, 23, 204
Peterson, Dr. Shailer, 117
Philippine Islands, 114
Phoenix, Ariz., 46, 149
Pilgrims, 17
Pima Indians, 14, 38–46
Pine Ridge Sioux Indians, 75–77, 118
Plagues, 17
Point 4 Program, 197–200
Portland Oregonian, 145
Powell, J. W., 203
Powhatan Confederacy, 93
Presbyterian Church, 73
Preston, Scott, 180–81
Provinse, John, 193
Public Health Service, U.S., 101, 172
Pueblo Indians, 83, 94, 174, 175
Pueblo Lands Board, 83
Pueblo Relief Act (1933), 130

Quakers, 49, 88
Qualla Reservation, 168

Ray, Verne F., 140
Reclamation Bureau, U.S., 40
"Recognition of Cultural Diversities in the Postwar World" (Benedict), 194–95
Red Cross, 115
Reservations, 15, 20, 35 ff., 62, 66, 67, 82, 93, 104, 189
    Alaska, 125–27
    Eastern Band of Cherokees, 168–73
    Klamath, 139–40
    legal status, 161–64
    Navajo, 176–88
    Pima, 39–46, 75
    Pine Ridge Sioux, 75–77

Sisseton Sioux, 77
    Turtle Mountain, 158–61
Resettlement Administration, 102
Resident Populations on Indian Reservations, 1950, 18
Revolutionary War, 51–52, 57
Rhodes, Charles J., 88–90, 102, 115
Rio Grande Pueblo Indians, 174, 175
Riverside, Calif., 149
Roberts, W. O., 167
Roosevelt, Franklin D., 25, 94
Rosenthal, Joe, 44
Royal Proclamation (1763), 51
Russia, 94, 126
Ryan, John A., 94
Ryan W. Carson, Jr., 115, 118

Sac Indians, 192–93
Safford Valley, Ariz., 40
Salt Lake City, Utah, 149
Samoa, 114
San Carlos, Ariz., 149
San Juan River, 185
Sand Creek massacre, 35–36
Santa Fe Railroad, 55
Sapir, Edward, 23, 203
Scattergood, J. Henry, 88, 102, 115
Schools, see Education
Schurz, Carl, 72
Schuyler, Maj. Gen. Philip, 52
Selective Service Act, 183
Sells, Cato, 81
Seminole Indians, 19, 93, 109
Senate, 59, 62, 67, 73, 126–27, 180, 197, 200
    Civil Service Committee, 133–34
    Committee on Indian Affairs, 94, 116, 141–43, 180
    Report 310, 124–25
Sequoya (Cherokee), 30
Shaw, Helen Louise, quoted, 49–50
Sheridan, Gen. Philip H., 73
Sherman, Gen. William T., 36, 176
Shipley, David L., 182
Shoshone Indians, 55
Sioux Indians, 72, 75–77, 93, 118
Sisseton Sioux Indians, 77
Six Nations (Iroquois), 52
Smith, Caleb B., 66

Smith, Edward P., 67
Smithsonian Institution, 102
Soil Conservation Service, 101–2, 104
Southern Review, 34
Spain, 39, 175
Stanford University Research Institute, 144
Stockbridge Indians, 108
Sun dance, 14
Supreme Court, 28, 31, 54–56, 105, 111, 120–21, 127

Tama, Iowa, 192
Tax, Sol, 19, 156, 192–93
Technical Cooperation-Bureau of Indian Affairs, 104
Teller, Henry M., 72–73, 74, 138
Tennessee, University of, 171
Thomas, William H., 168
Thompson, Jacob, 66
Tocqueville, Count Alexis de, 59–60
Trade and Intercourse Act (1834), 64, 189–90
Treaties, 30, 59, 64, 66–67, 70, 91–92, 97, 105, 108, 126, 176, 177, 180, 181, 190
Tribal Business Committee, 141
Truman, Harry S., 184
Tsali Institute, 171
Tuba City, Ariz., 183
Turtle Mountain Band, 158–61
Tuscarora Indians, 52, 108

United States as Guardian of Hualapai v. *Santa Fe Pacific Railroad Company* (1941), 55–56
United States Indian Training and Industrial School, 110
United States v. *Alcea Band of Tillamooks* (1946), 127
United States v. *Shoshone Tribe* (1938), 55
Unto These Hills (pageant), 171
Urban League, 155
Ute Indians, 14

Uto-Aztecan-Tanoan language group, 23, 204

Vattel, Emmerich von, 30
Villard, Oswald Garrison, 94
Virginia Company, 107
Voegelin, C. F., 203

Wales, 22
Walker, Francis A., 48
War Department, 61, 62, 64–65, 115, 195
War of 1812, 92
War Relocation Authority, 150
Warne, William E., 199–200
Washington, D.C., 46, 47, 63
Washington, George, 52, 53
Watkins, Arthur V., 141
Western Monthly Review, 34–35
Wheeler, Burton K., 95
Wheeler-Howard Act, *see* Indian Reorganization Act
Wheelock, Eleazar, 107
Whipple, Bishop H. B., 35
Willard, John, 156
Williams, Roger, 26
Wilson, James, 52
Window Rock, Ariz., 182
Winthrop, John, 71
Woolman, John, 49
Worcester, Samuel, 32
Worcester v. *Georgia* (1832), 54–55, 120–21
Work, Hubert, 83
World War 1, 76, 115
World War II, 24, 101, 149–50, 179–80, 183–84
Writing, 26, 30

Yankton Sioux Indians, 72

Zimmerman, William, Jr., 116–17, 133–34, 186
Zuni Indians, 118, 174